MATT

Happiness the inside job

THE 7 WAYS TO LIFE-CHANGING HAPPINESS

CABIN PRESS

British Library Cataloguing in Publication Data.
A catalogue record for this book is available from the British Library.

EDITED by Debs Syron
DESIGN & ILLUSTRATIONS by denisholzmueller.de

© All artwork and illustrations are copyright
by Matt Pepper and Denis Holzmüller

CABIN PRESS
10 Harley Street
London W1G 9PF

ISBN Paperback: 978-1-9998803-3-0
ISBN E-book: 978-1-9998803-9-2

First printed 2018

For Tasha and my little Peppers

. . .

To my anonymous sponsor
thank you for launching my dream
all those years ago

CONTENTS

WHERE DOES HAPPINESS HANG OUT?

WAY 1 FIRE UP YOUR OWN HAPPINESS

WAY 2 EXPOSE YOUR TA-DAA

WAY 3 TEND YOUR EMOTIONAL GARDEN

WAY 4 JUMP ON THE GROOVY TRAIN OF THOUGHT

WAY 5 LISTEN TO YOUR WISE OLD GUT

WAY 6 TURN YOUR 'MUCK' TO LUCK

WAY 7 PIMP UP YOUR PURPOSE

YOU ARE A HAPPINESS-GENERATING MACHINE

Where does happiness hang out?

The journey of a seeker

I've always been a bit of a seeker by nature, wanting to get to the bottom of this thing called "happiness". Twenty years ago I began my journey to understand what happiness is and how to harness it, and along the way I discovered that not only is it possible for everyone to find true happiness, but that it is one of our fundamental birthrights.

As with everyone, my life has been a journey of ups and downs, stresses and strains, good and bad times. I have always known somewhere inside me that it must be possible to be happy despite all this, so I set out to discover how I could make myself happy. I asked myself questions about life and happiness, determined to find out how it worked. Was happiness just a random stroke of luck, or was it determined by factors such as family, upbringing, success, earnings, job, status and having friends or a partner?

How was it that some days I could wake up happy and ready to enjoy myself, and then the next I would find it a struggle? What was going on?

Why was I feeling so changeable when nothing was particularly different in my life?

I had always been a fairly happy guy by nature, but it began to seem like my happiness was a bit reactionary and random. My good feelings seemed to fluctuate depending on lots of factors: how I was being treated; whether I was enjoying my work or not; what was happening in my day; if things were going well with my family; if things were turning out as I wanted them to, or even simply if the sun was shining. In short, I felt like a leaf blown about in the wind, not remotely in charge of my own happiness. I didn't want to continue to feel trapped by my circumstances so I asked myself a question…

Is there a better way to live a more fulfilled life?

My personal journey through life had certainly thrown me a few tough experiences to deal with over the years: from my parents divorcing during my childhood, family upsets, bereavements, stressful relationships and a bout of ill health, I had had my fair share of challenges to face.

Despite this I didn't want to just sit back and let life happen to me, I wanted to go looking for answers, in fact I felt driven to find answers. I began going on courses, visiting therapists and listening to psychologists. Some of it worked and was relevant, and some didn't, but gradually I began to gather the tools I needed to find my way through life. It was a process of trial and error.

During this process my primary motivation was to find happiness for myself. However I was also incredibly driven by my work as a practitioner wanting to improve my clients' health and happiness. I wanted to be the kind of practitioner who walked the walk, not one who simply talked the talk saying, "Do this, it will help you to be happy". It was clear that first I had to feel happy myself.

Throughout my twenty years of professional work I have heard countless people's dreams, struggles and aspirations. On paper many of them would appear to have it all so how could they be unhappy? I have treated CEOs who have great wealth, beautiful houses, lavish holidays, loving spouses and children... why were they unhappy? I have worked with mums who had the children they wanted, interesting jobs, nice houses... why were they unhappy? Even celebrity clients with adoring fans, travelling the world, being treated like royalty, were still unhappy.

In every case, from students to millionaires, from those longing not to be single, to those wishing not to be married, unemployed to overworked; no matter what a person's circumstances, most of my clients seemed unable to find their inner happiness. I wanted to get to the bottom of why this was.

I will be happy when...

A common theme from both my own life and those of my clients, was to be in the state of continually waiting for the future to magically bring us happiness, with the belief that, "I will be happy when…"

I will be happy when…

… my relationship improves or I start a new one
… I get a promotion or a better job
… someone starts loving me in the way that I want
… I reach my target (weight, fitness, etc)
… I get a bigger house
… I buy myself a Ferrari
… I win the lottery or simply have more money
… I get those new shoes
… the weekend arrives

In this way happiness is always waiting just around the corner. If life would just do me a favour and line up as I want it to, **then** I would be happy. Being in a constant state of longing, wishing, waiting or even resenting never seems to work very well. The future is not a very reliable thing to hang one's happiness on!

Another problem was becoming apparent. Even when the object of our desire arrived in our lives i.e. we got the thing that we promised ourselves would make us happy, we often realised that this wasn't the case. For so many of my clients, even when they got the new car, new partner or new job they had been longing for, they were still not happy.

For many, the feeling of happiness didn't seem to last.

I began to realise that happiness was not a fixed entity that depended on stuff, relationships, status, money, achievements, the past, or the future. Of course parts of all of the above could enhance people's lives, but where was true happiness hanging out? I was determined to find out.

I'm feeling more myself again

After my first few years in practice I began to notice that, although clients would initially come to see me for help with a physical ailment, once I had taken the history and nature of their health complaint, whether it was a skin condition, stomach complaint, hormonal imbalance or sleep problem, we would then move on to talk about how they felt in themselves and their current life situation. This is when an interesting common theme began to emerge.

This theme usually seemed to involve some sort of stress or personal unhappiness that they were experiencing. I noticed that the more we worked on addressing their emotional state and improving their sense of personal happiness, the better they felt, and as a result their physical problems would clear up too.

Do I believe that there is a link between our emotional state of mind and our physical health? Yes certainly, I've seen it too many times. However, seeing so much unhappiness led me to a further question…

Why were people feeling lost, overwhelmed, unhappy, depressed or simply stuck in the first place?

This is when my work got really interesting.

The more I worked with people to address and remove their stresses and negative states of mind, helping them to feel better and get back to feeling good again, the more they would start coming in to their sessions saying…

"Thanks so much, I'm feeling more myself again"

And when I asked, "How does that feel?"

Invariably the reply would be, **"Good, really good!"**

As more and more people came in with this feeling of being more themselves again, I would ask them to describe it to me. Commonly they would use words such as:

Calm   Relaxed

Alive   Happy

Powerful   Clearer

In charge   Free

What became clear to me was that underneath all the stress, worry and negativity, there was always a more natural, happier place within us. This place feels good to people; it feels calm, centred, more peaceful, as if this is a totally natural way to be. It is a place which feels good; this is our natural state.

I had experienced this on my own journey, when I began to take responsibility for my own happiness. The more I acknowledged my own natural, happier place the more happiness I began to feel. What I realised was that when people are being themselves they feel good. Conversely when they aren't being themselves they aren't able to feel good.

What a fantastic internal feedback system we have!

Make feeling good the cornerstone

F eeling good should be the most important aspect of our lives. In fact what I realised is that feeling good should be the cornerstone of our lives because it influences everything that we are and do.

Feeling good improves our ability to deal with stress, our levels of health, our mindset and our ability to see things more clearly, which in turn shapes our future, enabling us to go for what we want in life. It is fair to say that all aspects of our lives are improved when we are feeling good… it is the best place to be.

Here are some of the benefits of feeling good:

Life runs smoother
… We have more energy
… Things don't get to us as much
… Life's niggles just bounce off us
… We don't concern ourselves with what is not important
… We let others get on with their lives

… We feel more carefree and more able
to have fun

We get inspired
… Our mindsets are clearer
… We have more clarity with better ideas
and actions
… We see the best in ourselves and others

Our family lives are better
… Our relationships are easier and more fun
… Our relationships with our partners, siblings,
children are more loving
… We are more engaged and happier with
family life

We are happier at work
… Work ideas and creativity flow more freely
and are more enjoyable
… We are more engaged with others
… We are more productive
… We are less stressed and more resilient
… We can listen more easily
… We get in our "zone"

Our health improves
… Our sense of wellbeing is improved
… Our stress levels reduce dramatically
… Health problems decrease
… We are more connected to our friends,
family and society in general

The positive side of feeling bad

In this quest to find out how to feel good, what I realised was that negative states of mind are not who we are, as real and as intense as they may feel, but simply reactions to circumstances, and an indicator that we have moved away from our natural state.

I learnt that we need to pay attention to how we are feeling at all times, as our feelings are our guidance, giving constant feedback. If we aren't feeling good, something needs to be addressed. It's a bit like driving along a motorway and beginning to drift onto the rumble strip, it feels bumpy and is alerting us that something is wrong. In the same way this uncomfortable feeling is showing us that we are going off course.

When negative feelings strike
we can ask ourselves…

'What do I really want?'

'Why is this uncomfortable?'

'What needs to be addressed or changed within me here?'

By beginning to see our negative feelings as tools to guide us, not as problems in themselves, we can begin to take control of our lives. This is not always easy, but it is certainly possible when we have the courage and desire for things to change. With practice we can quickly stop ourselves from getting stuck in a negative state and instead use it to guide us back on track.

The good news is that this whole book is about how to do just that!

Learning to feel good again

One of my key philosophies is that learning to feel good can make a dramatic difference to our experience of life. It can indeed change our lives. Feeling good is the indicator we are looking for, to guide us to the life-changing happiness we dream of.

So here is the question…

What do I need to do to learn to feel good again?

It is my hope that this book will give you the tools to find your own true and lasting happiness, every day. We will go back to the basics of the real reasons for happiness and more importantly, how you can get there. We will learn that it is possible to move forwards, and create the life-changing happiness we desire.

As we go through the book, I have outlined what I have found to be the key factors which can help us move forwards and achieve a happy and fulfilled life. I will explain all of the concepts that I have found and seen work. With any tools like these, it takes both understanding and then application to see what a difference they can make, but stick with it, it will be so worthwhile.

You may find that one or two chapters work really well for you now, and that others will work better in the future. They all have the potential to help you to a better-feeling place; this is the place from which your life will change.

The 7 ways to life-changing happiness

I want to show you how you can deal with any problems in a new and empowering way. I want to show you how you can create a different and more exciting future for yourself. I want to show you how to create a happy mindset and the key aspects to being a happy fulfilled person. Whatever your starting place, I believe this possible for everyone.

I'm not a fan of complicated ideas or analysis and prefer a much simpler, easy to understand approach. I have found this works best for me. With the help of a few simple steps, well 7 that I have found, your life can and will be changed.

To whet your appetite on how I am going to help you feel good, here is a summary of my 7 ways to life-changing happiness:

1. Fire up your own happiness

How you can be in charge of how happy you are and find ways to raise yourself up The Happiness Barometer. See how life improves dramatically by learning to feel good in yourself first. Say goodbye to believing that circumstances have to dictate how you feel. You have the power to change how you are feeling.

2. Expose your Ta Daa!

How you can be the 'real you' again. Let's get you being the person you were born to be. Placing this crucial piece of the happiness puzzle in place by living life as your brilliant self, expressing your uniqueness, being able to 'dump any fronts' which you thought you needed to function. You can now be happy in your own shoes.

3. Tend your emotional garden

How you can nurture and grow your own positive emotions, doing what it takes to feel your best and weeding out any unwanted negative emotions. You have the power to improve how you feel.

You might feel bad or even get low, but I am going to help you see how you can improve things emotionally for yourself and quickly fire up your own good mood.

4. Jump on The Groovy Train of Thought

You can fill your mind with good-feeling happy thoughts and stop allowing it to get clogged up with negative ones. Learning to "think great" is a game changer. You can change both the way you think, and what you think, so you become in charge of your own better thoughts. Let's get you learning to enjoy and feel empowered by your own thoughts.

5. Listen to your wise old gut

Learn to follow your gut and know what is right for you. Let's get you tuning in and really listening to what your wise old gut is telling you, because it always knows what is best. This way your best life possible will unfold naturally.

6. Turn your 'muck' to luck

Learn to bounce back from the worst of times and create your own best of times. We look at the keys to self-empowerment and how you can achieve an empowered state of mind to take you over life's hurdles and move your life forwards. Let's get you creating a clear calm perspective on what your life is all about and seeing the best in people, situations and your future.

7. Pimp up your purpose

How you can point your life in the right direction and get to where you want to be. By doing what makes you feel good and discovering your passions, you will be inspired to jump out of bed each day to follow your dreams.

Fire up your own happiness

WAY 1

Feel good and see what happens

When my clients tell me that their relationship is in tatters, that they don't like their job, that they have nothing to look forward to, that everything seems difficult, the solution is usually very simple. I say...

Let's get you feeling good first and then see what happens

This can be puzzling for many people, who believe that only a change in their external circumstances will make them happier. Don't get me wrong, releasing yourself from a bad relationship or awful job can be very liberating, but I like to look at it differently. You see, changing your circumstances doesn't always create happiness, it simply changes your circumstances. Learning to feel good in yourself is what makes the difference.

I have developed a tool to explain this concept called, The Happiness Barometer.

23

The Happiness Barometer

T he Happiness Barometer is a visual tool which quickly and easily allows us to identify how we are feeling. This can be how we are feeling at a particular moment in time, or it can relate to our general state of happiness.

It seems obvious when looking at The Happiness Barometer, but it is surprising how actually reading some of the key indicators can focus our minds, telling us immediately where we are currently at with our happiness level.

We may find that we travel up and down The Happiness Barometer over the course of a day, a week, a month, or suddenly when reacting to a new situation. Usually people have a place where they would say they could be found most of the time. If some good things happen they might go up, or if something not so good happens they might slide down again, but generally they could identify where they normally are.

How are you feeling
on The Happiness Barometer?

Feeling	How you are experiencing life
Great	Feeling on top of the world Life flows easily Energy is high Full of good ideas and creativity High resilience to problems Moving forwards easily Excited by the future In a loving place High self-love and self-nurture Your future path opens up in front of you
Good	Feeling good Life has good times Energy good Ideas good
Ok	Life feels ok Getting by Some good days, some tricky days Energy ok Getting on with things ok
Not Good	Life feels like a struggle Energy low Difficulties in moving forward Dwelling on problems
Despair	Feeling what's the point? Anxiousness Life seems difficult or pointless Mood feels black or dark Feeling separate to others Loss of confidence Can't move forwards Low self-love and self-nurture Life seems to be shutting down Feeling overwhelmed

Thoughts match feelings

A nother interesting link which I have noticed is that the quality of our feelings seems to match our thinking. Here are some examples of this:

Feeling	Thoughts
Great	Excited and positive Anything is possible Free-flowing ideas Have great clarity and creativity Find solutions easily Look for and see the best in people and things
Good	Ideas and creativity good Positive outlook and mindset
Ok	Dealing with situations Average coping ideas
Not Good	Negative views and worries Difficulties in moving forward Dwelling on things Stuck in a bit of a rut
Despair	Helpless thoughts Paranoid and dark thoughts Stuck powerless thoughts

When we feel good, we think good thoughts.
It is so important to remember this point, as how we are thinking often dictates how happy we feel.

Same place, different face

T his theory of travelling up and down The Happiness Barometer is all well and good, but how does it actually work in practice? Let's take a look at some examples of it in action…

The 'no milk in the fridge' moment

Scenario A

Feeling
I wake up in a bad mood, feeling 'Not Good' on The Happiness Barometer.

Situation
I go to the fridge to get some milk for my morning bowl of cereal but we have run out.

Result
In my head I shout, "Argh, there's no milk left!! I was desperate for a bowl of cornflakes and now I can't have it!". I feel aggravated and upset, especially today of all days as there is so much going on.

Scenario B

Feeling
I wake up in a good mood, feeling 'Good' or 'Great' on The Happiness Barometer.

Situation
I go to the fridge to get some milk for my morning bowl of cereal but we have run out.

Result
In my head I say, "Ah, no milk… what shall I do now? OK, I will drink juice instead, and maybe have some toast to tide me over until I get to work. Actually I have been meaning to try out a new coffee shop next to work, and this a great opportunity to treat myself."

Same place, different face

In the second scenario, because I began the morning feeling happier, I see the situation in a whole new way. I am now pleased that there wasn't any milk. I am happy, making new choices and excited by what is coming up for me in the breakfast department!

It may be a trivial example but it shows that our experience of life is directly affected by where we are hanging out on The Happiness Barometer. Here are another couple of examples of situations which I have experienced with my clients…

In need of a desert island

One of my clients who was in his early forties was under huge pressure at work, he had a demanding boss, and long working hours had left him feeling completely overwhelmed. He came to me saying he needed to leave his job because he had nothing left in the tank to give. He was so stressed that he was even considering leaving his wife and children, he felt he couldn't give them what they needed and whatever they asked him for simply wound him up and made him feel guilty. He just wanted to be left alone and move to a desert island.

Clearly he wasn't in a great place, he was at the 'Despair' end of The Happiness Barometer and wasn't feeling good at all. He was having very negative thoughts about himself and his life in general.

I said to him the same thing I so often say to my clients…

Let's get you feeling good first and then see what happens

We worked together for two months getting him to feel better in himself, whilst still in the same job, and still at home with his family.

The result was that he began to enjoy his job again and subsequently got promoted. He began to feel happier in himself and appreciated his wife and children more, which allowed him to find more time and energy to spend with them. He was happier and more confident, and therefore able to approach life in a whole new way.

Same place, different face

Again the circumstances hadn't changed. What had changed was how he felt inside, which in turn gave him a new perspective. By finding ways to move up The Happiness Barometer his life had changed for the better.

I can't live with my husband anymore

Another client in her mid-thirties came to see me because she was going through divorce proceedings with her husband. It was nobody's fault and their separation was amicable, but due to financial circumstances they were still living in the same house, until it sold and they could go their separate ways. She was anxious, tired, isolated and agitated. She hated going home and felt she couldn't be in the same room as her husband. Everything about him annoyed her and she felt she just couldn't carry on with this living arrangement. She was very tearful and stuck at the lowest level, 'Despair', on The Happiness Barometer.

She came to see me in complete turmoil desperate for a way out of her circumstances. As is often the case it wasn't her physical circumstances that were the problem, it was her state of mind that needed to change. Again I said…

Let's get you feeling good first and then see what happens

She had lost herself in always trying to please others, and that coupled with a feeling of loneliness within an unhappy marriage meant her self confidence was at rock bottom. We worked together for a few months and gradually she began to take the reins of her life into her own hands. She began to be true to herself for the first time.

Her happiness improved and she began to feel freer. As she began to feel better, so her relationship with her husband improved. They began talking openly again, were able to have family dinners for the sake of their children and co-habited in a friendly way until they sold the house and went their separate ways.

Same place, different face

By moving up The Happiness Barometer to feeling good in herself, her life had changed. She improved how she was feeling on the inside. She became happier, less anxious and her newly found strength meant she was now in the driving seat.

Moving on up

These examples show just how important it is to feel better in yourself before anything else can improve. If we are at the bottom end of The Happiness Barometer, life seems difficult and at times impossible. Decisions don't come easily and it is likely that we will feel very stressed and negative.

When we move up towards the top of The Happiness Barometer we can find a new perspective, strength arrives and life becomes a whole lot easier. In this place we often find that good things begin to happen, we have more energy which allows us to glide more easily through life, dealing with stress like a knife through butter.

As we near the top of The Happiness Barometer great things start to happen. Life blossoms, health problems reduce or go away naturally and relationships flourish. The feeling is one of riding high, with self esteem blooming, ideas flowing and creativity maximized. Other people will sense the difference and be drawn in by our positive energy.

In this state we feel like we have the Midas touch, everything seems to fall into place. We can enjoy ourselves, our lives and everything in between. This is the place to aim for and I want to show you how to fire yourself up there!

I strongly believe that everyone can get to this great place, because it is an internal, not an external process. Wherever you are starting from you can find a way. You can get back to feeling better again. I've seen it happen time and time again.

We don't need things to alter, situations to change, or people to behave differently. They might do, due to changes within you, or you may decide that you want to make changes, but you don't need things to change to feel better.

If we can change how we are feeling, then we can change the lens through which we view life. The goal is not just to feel happier for a few minutes or a few hours, but rather to aim for days, weeks, months and hopefully years of happiness and fulfilment. Obviously it is impossible to stay on top at all times; when life throws things at us we will fluctuate up and down, but if we can consciously try to get to the top of The Happiness Barometer and stay there, despite the ups and downs, we will be all the happier.

Realising that happiness is an "Inside Job" not based on external factors is the first way to life-changing happiness.

You are in charge

Realising that you are in charge is where the power lies, you truly can fire yourself up there.

WAY 1
Fire up your own happiness

·BAROMETER RISING TIPS·

Learn to feel good in yourself,
then life will change for the better

Whatever your starting place,
you can fire yourself up
The Happiness Barometer

Happiness is an 'inside job' and
not based on external factors

Try to make choices and decisions
when you are feeling good

The best things in life happen
when you feel good!

Expose your Ta-Daa

WAY 2

Born to be you

T he moment we are born, we are born to be our own brilliant selves. We arrive in the world saying, "Ta-Daa! Here I am! This is me! Bring it on!"

We arrive ready for the world, with our own unique blend of characteristics and personality traits which make us each our own individual person. We arrive, a bundle of potential setting out to experience the world as the person we were meant to be.

I was born to be me and you were born to be you

In my view this is so important because it goes a long way towards explaining why people will or will not feel good in their lives. Whether we are feeling good or not is not random or merely a coincidence. We must tune into something much more fundamental to recognise our natural state, where we are able to be ourselves.

Let's illustrate this a little more…

The orchestra theory

T his theory shows how we are meant to be as humans, and it can even give us an insight into the reasons why we may, or may not, be feeling good.

Let's consider an orchestra. We know that it is made up of a whole host of different instruments: from violins to trumpets, cellos to trombones, clarinets to tambourines, an orchestra has everything from the humble triangle to the kettle drum.

Each instrument is unique having its own size, shape and sound. It is equally able to play alone or as part of a group, making sounds in exactly the way it was designed to perform. An orchestra is built by each instrument being uniquely itself, but also all coming together to make one beautiful harmonious piece of music. Each instrument plays its part as and when it's needed, with its own different quality and styles.

So how does this relate to us humans?

Just as the instruments are unique, we humans

are completely unique too. We each have our own abilities, qualities and characteristics. Humans differ in so many ways with our individual skills, opinions, desires and personalities. The important thing is that we are each allowed to express these characteristics in our own way.

The key to this is that just as an orchestra is made up of a multitude of different instruments, each adding its qualities to create a piece of music... so each person also makes up part of the human race, by bringing to the world what they uniquely have to offer as themselves. If everyone can play their part as themselves then it will work in perfect harmony.

Trumpets don't try to be violins

T aking the orchestra theory a step further, let's think about one individual instrument, for example, the trumpet. A trumpet, as we know, has its own qualities and sounds.

• The trumpet doesn't try to be a violin, it is happy doing its thing as intended.

• The trumpet doesn't deliberately play out of tune or detune itself in order for other instruments to feel better.

• The trumpet doesn't try to mould itself into being another instrument like a violin, trying to become a 'trumolin', believing that this will make it perform better.

• The trumpet doesn't hide its brilliance, it is happy to proudly play its part in the orchestra.

In the same way, humans must make it their goal to fully be who they were meant to be. In reality we rarely do. So often we try to alter ourselves to be

42

something else, something different, something we are not. Why do we do this? Here are some common reasons:

- Trying to fit in

- Trying to please others

- Trying to keep the equilibrium

- Trying to mould ourselves to be like someone else

- Trying to meet other people's expectations

What happens if the trumpet tries to be a violin?

Well it would look like this:

It would not be much use to itself or to the orchestra.

What happens when we try to be something we are not, and start moving away from who we are meant to be?

When we try to be something we are not, it doesn't feel good

This is a key piece of the happiness puzzle. We have to be ourselves to feel good, anything else just doesn't work. Not being ourselves takes us down The Happiness Barometer. Conversely 'being who we are' takes us up.

Dump the front

H ave you ever felt you needed to put on a front for friends, family or at work, in order to get through a situation? I know I have. We create a front when at some point in our lives we decide that being ourselves is not good enough, or simply isn't going to work. So we create a front, a persona, to do the job for us.

In one way creating a front can be a very useful tool, helping us to get through a variety of tricky situations. These fronts are often created as learnt behaviour in childhood when we may feel vulnerable. As we grow into adulthood they are less necessary to survive, but we often think that we still need them. Putting on a front is not always a bad thing, however often our lives would be much better and far happier without feeling the need to do this.

There are two main problems with this coping strategy:

1. It doesn't feel right; we can never feel totally happy when we are putting on a front

2. It is emotionally draining; we can't help but feel tired after having to put on a front

Fronts are never satisfying, they need to be dumped!

As we have already mentioned in the previous chapter 'feeling good' is the key guidance system here. Many of my clients have said that they don't know who they are anymore. They have forgotten who they really are, because they are too busy concentrating on trying to be what they believe others want them to be.

These issues can be easily resolved if you remember one simple thing…

Who you actually are is never far away

Your true self is like a friendly runner keeping up alongside you, whichever path in life you take. Once you decide to step across into the version of yourself that is truly you, you will begin to feel better. Even just having the thought that soon you will be you again, can make us feel better.

Dumping the front isn't instant, it is a process. As we go through the book we will be learning ways to get happier simply by being ourselves. The more we get happier being ourselves, the less we will need to put on a front.

Moving out of sync

There are three key things that happen when we move out of sync with the person we were meant to be:

1. Confidence begins to lessen

True confidence comes when we feel truly ourselves, we are sure in our own shoes. So it makes sense that as we move away from this place, we begin to feel less confident. As we move away from being the person we were meant to be, and start becoming more of what we are not, our confidence begins to subside.

True confidence is actually quite a calm state of mind, it is in no way forceful or arrogant.

Arrogance and forcefulness are usually symptomatic of someone who is not confident and is therefore trying to compensate for this fact.

2. Emptiness arrives

As we move away from the person we were meant to be, we begin to feel a sense of emptiness.

Interestingly, this emptiness is actually created from the void between these two versions of ourselves. This makes sense because when we feel ourselves, we feel full and alive. When we move away from this and start not being ourselves we feel empty.

In my experience, when people have this empty feeling inside, they seek to fill it with a multitude of activities to try to fill the void. Here are a few examples:

- Smoking
- Overeating
- Overworking
- Taking drugs
- Addiction to social media
- Drinking too much alcohol
- Allowing destructive relationships to continue

Strangely enough these are all ways of people trying to feel better again, but none of these things will ever make us feel better in the long run. Getting back to being our true selves is the only real answer.

3. We begin to feel inner sadness, low or even depressed

As we begin to move away from the person we were meant to be, it creates an inner sadness because deep down we know that we just want to be ourselves. There are several other reasons for feeling low or depressed, but in my experience this is one of the main ones.

So now we have a combination of lowered confidence, a sense of emptiness and a feeling of inner sadness. This is not a happy place to find ourselves but sadly it is an all too common one.

It all sounds pretty miserable at this point doesn't it?

Fortunately there is good news; all of the above are totally reversible. Of course you can be yourself, and of course you can get back to who you were meant to be. There is one surefire way of knowing that you are heading in the right direction, and that is simply that you will begin to feel good again!

Hitting the sweet spot

B eing true to yourself feels good, it takes you up The Happiness Barometer. This is the indicator that we need to guide us through life, to the point of our greatest happiness. We were born to feel good, to have fun and enjoy ourselves, able to be and express everything that we have to offer. That surely is the whole point of life?

The interesting part is what happens when we **can** be ourselves, 'get into sync' and start to feel better. Our lives begin to take off in new and exciting ways, work issues turn out well, relationships improve, ideas arrive and take shape and we become clearer in purpose and direction. Everything seems to suddenly fall into place, all because we began to simply be ourselves. This is what I refer to as hitting the sweet spot and I have seen it happen time and time again.

Getting back to the 'real you' is so important to create life-changing happiness. Decide that now is the right time to be you again. Being yourself is about feeling good in your own shoes, finding your authentic self and coming back to being you again.

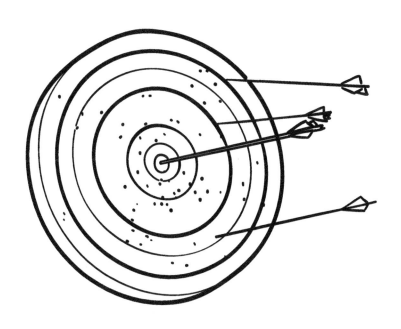

WAY 2
Expose your Ta-Daa

·BAROMETER RISING TIPS·

Be your brilliant self

Express your uniqueness

Don't detune yourself

Dump your front and
enjoy being you

Stay in-sync with who you are

Now is the time to come
back to the 'real you'

Be happy in your own shoes

Tend your emotional garden

WAY 3

Emotional gardening

W hat does it take to make my emotions feel better, feel good and stay happy? This is a question I used to ask myself on a regular basis. I used to believe that my emotions were random, dependent on external situations and it was only by chance that I would feel better on some days and worse on others.

Now I have changed my tune. I have to be very active in attending to my own emotions if I want to feel happy. It is a proactive job that requires attention and a lot of practice.

The best gardeners keep a close eye on what is happening in their gardens, tending to them day to day. They make sure they only have the plants, shrubs, fruit, vegetables and trees that they want to have growing there. They work to create the right environment by nurturing the soil and giving the plants the nourishment they need to grow and flourish. They are quick to act on anything unwanted; weeds, pests or overgrown areas are eliminated in order to avoid the gardens being taken over.

The same goes for our emotional health. It is time to create the positive emotions we want to feel, nurture our happy states to help them grow and flourish, and weed out the unwanted negative emotions as soon as possible.

The overgrown garden

Overgrown and full of unwanted feelings such as sadness, frustration, anger, jealously, hate, despair. With the odd bit of happiness here and there this garden has been overrun by negative emotions.

The happy garden

This garden is full of positive feelings such as happiness, freedom, contentment, joy and liveliness.

Life is not about having a perfect happy emotional garden all the time, as we all know. It will always throw us a situation or two to deal with, whether that is at work, in our relationships, with our health or at home. What we can do is learn how to cultivate a better-feeling place within ourselves, nurture our positive emotions and prevent the negative emotions from running riot by weeding them out.

We can plant the seeds of positive emotion that we want to have, then actively nurture and help them to grow. These positive happy emotions will thrive as long as we take good care of them. We have to get more proactive about growing and nurturing the positive feelings we want to feel.

Negative emotions, like sadness, jealousy, hate and despair, can grow only if we let them take hold. We have to be like a vigilant gardener, quickly spotting that negative feelings are beginning to grow and taking action to remove them.

We choose which emotions grow in our emotional garden, good and bad

By tending to our emotional garden we are proactively making ourselves as emotionally strong and resilient as we can. When we feel strong and able to cope, happiness springs forwards and life takes off. This happier emotional garden enables us to get through life's challenges much more easily and to grow our positive emotions and life experiences.

We all have the power to create beautiful vibrant emotional gardens simply by tending to how good we feel as much as possible. If we do, we will go up The Happiness Barometer.

So how do we achieve the perfect emotional garden? I found the answers were never complicated but certainly needed practice. Below are a few techniques which may help you.

Don't bottle it up

I n all my years working with clients, one of the most common traits affecting people's emotional health is the 'bottling up' of emotions.

Bottling up can be defined as holding back what you are feeling about a situation or refusing to deal with something that is on your mind.

Bottling up means keeping it in

By keeping feelings inside we lock away the emotions related to the situation. But where do the feelings go? Can we just ignore them?

I would say not.

I believe these feelings stay within us, and if left unattended can lead to health problems both physically and mentally. Either way this will work against us in our quest to feel good. Bottling up is therefore never a good idea for our health.

Emotional balloon theory

H ere is a child's modelling balloon, the kind which is made into fantastic shapes such as swords or dogs at children's birthday parties.

The balloon can be used to illustrate how the body, emotions and mind react when we bottle up our emotions.

The body, mind and emotions are linked in the 3 sections of the balloon in the following way:

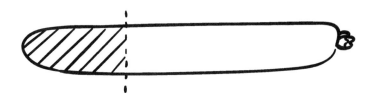

The Left Side = Physical Health
This represents the physical health and symptoms of the body and how well it functions

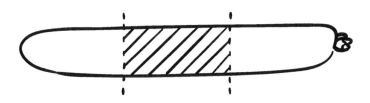

The Middle = Emotional Health
This represents how we are feeling

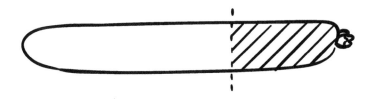

The Right Side = Mental Health
This represents how we are thinking and analysing our lives (stresses and anxieties etc)

In a healthy state all three areas are balanced and in equal proportion, our physical body, emotions and mind are all playing ball nicely. We are dealing with, and reacting to, life very well.

Just look at what happens though if, for example, something traumatic occurs. Perhaps someone has lost their job, a relationship has ended, there has been a breakdown in a family relationship or even the loss of a loved one.

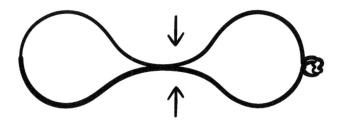

Look at what happens to the middle of the balloon when the emotional area is suppressed and we bottle up emotionally; the middle gets squeezed in.

If we squeeze in this middle area of the balloon, the mechanics of it push both ends outwards and upwards. In doing so, this creates symptoms both in the left side (physical health) and the right side (mental health).

Common physical health problems which I have seen in my clinic resulting from people bottling up are: headaches and migraines, skin complaints, joint problems, hormonal imbalances and sleeping difficulties.

Symptoms of the mind which I have seen from people bottling up are: heightened levels of worry, anxiety, increased stress and irritableness, feeling overwhelmed and a generally more defensive approach to life.

Physical symptoms of bottling up

Often clients will give me a list of symptoms they are experiencing, for example: low energy, thyroid problems, skin ailments, stomach complaints, headaches or hormonal imbalances. At this point I always ask them to tell me what happened in the three to six months before their symptoms started. Interestingly 99% will tell me about a shock, difficult situation or trauma that has recently affected them.

The important thing to realise is that it is not the situation that is the problem, as difficult or painful as it may be, it is how they have reacted to it. There are reactions that help you, and reactions that create a problem and make you even more unhappy or stressed.

To illustrate this point consider how a child reacts to a mildly traumatic incident…

Imagine a 4 year old boy who has friends over to play. They are all running around the living room having loads of fun, chasing and laughing with each other. Suddenly the boy is not looking where he is going and he bashes his head on a dining table. He is not hurt too badly, but it is painful. With the pain and shock of this incident he starts crying. He cries and cries seeking comfort from his mother. He is expressing the hurt and shock of what has happened to him. However within a few minutes he is beginning to feel better, then a few minutes later he is up and off, playing with his friends again, completely back on track.

The sequence was:

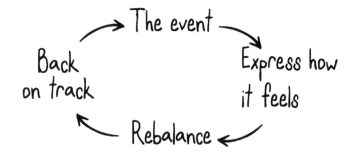

For many adults however, if they encounter a stressful event this sequence changes to:

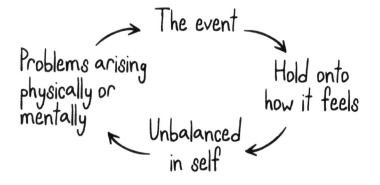

For different reasons many people learn to bottle up emotions instead of letting them out naturally. Here are some common reasons why people learn to bottle things from a young age:

- If someone's parents were not good at expressing their own emotions then they would not have been encouraged to do this either
- If someone was actively stopped from being emotional by an authority figure, such as a parent or a teacher, with the use of phrases such as, "Don't be a baby", "Big boys don't cry" or simply "Be quiet" when they tried to express themselves
- If someone was punished, sent to their room, or made to feel small in some way
- If someone was always told to, "Get on with it and be strong" especially with the British stiff upper lip mentality
- Some people simply feel unsafe or unsure how to show emotions; they are too shy to express themselves

Obviously 'not bottling up' shouldn't be taken to extremes. I am not saying we all have to become an emotional mess, but sharing our feelings with someone we trust is a step in the right direction and will certainly make us feel better.

Behavioural symptoms of bottling up

Apart from the physical symptoms I mentioned, I have also seen some tell-tale changes in behaviour too. One of the most common is that people start to make themselves extremely busy. They realise that if they give themselves any free-thinking time by slowing down, then they will have to deal with some uncomfortable feelings, so they keep busy instead. Often people don't even realise that they are doing this.

Busyness can take many forms:

- Inability to sit still or be idle
- Continual cleaning and tidying
- Higher than average TV/Radio consumption, sometimes even through the night
- Doing chores for others all the time, whilst putting yourself at bottom of the list
- Overworking
- Using escape tools like drinking, smoking, drug taking, overuse of social media and unhealthy relationships

You may identify with the above list and find that you have been keeping yourself busy. If you are now aware that you are doing this, then perhaps you can begin to make small changes to allow yourself more headspace, and put yourself at the top of your list for a change.

This is so important because bottling up leads to feeling bad, which takes us down The Happiness Barometer.

Emotional symptoms of bottling up

Feeling down
If you are bottling up, you can become full of negative feelings which have nowhere to go. The more this happens, the more likely you are to become depressed and withdrawn.

Loss of self confidence
In the second 'Way' we talked about the importance of 'being yourself'. By not expressing yourself, by which I mean showing how you are actually feeling, you are on some level not being who you are, which as we saw can lead to a loss of self-confidence.

See it as
a cleanse

H aving a healthy release for negative emotions is very important. Letting out these emotions is natural and cleansing for the soul. It is certainly not a sign of weakness. Quite the opposite. Getting rid of negative feelings can be incredibly liberating and rejuvenating.

However this is easier said than done for some people, especially those who have locked away how they are feeling for years, or even decades, relying on an 'I will keep going' mentality. Other people bottle up because they don't want to worry family and friends, or because they think others may not be interested, or they are simply too private to share these inner feelings and fears.

Trust your instinct with who you can talk to, choose a sympathetic friend or relation who is good at listening with empathy, or find professional help with a therapist. True friends don't mind hearing about your problems and being a sounding board to help you move forwards. Therapists are impartial and can give you a new perspective, which is sometimes easier as they have no vested interests or knowledge of you personally.

Being brave enough to get support can be a real help

If you don't want to say your problems or fears out loud, then writing a journal or just putting down how you are feeling on paper, can be a step in the right direction. I'm not saying that you must be a tearful mess whenever something happens, but you will find that if you can say it out loud or write it down, you will feel better as a result.

I found that sometimes I felt better being around others, yet other times being quiet on my own helped me to regroup. Unsurprisingly, women seem to be better at reaching out than men, but men are definitely getting better at opening up in our modern society.

Above all, be gentle and kind to yourself. This process is hard enough without giving yourself a hard time too.

Healthy expression can make all the difference to how we are feeling. As we go through this book and learn to feel better in ourselves, being able to speak about emotions will become much easier.

As we move up The Happiness Barometer we feel

less 'emotional', that is to say we become less sensitive to the smaller things that used to upset us. We also become much more resilient in life generally. When we feel better in ourselves life can be very different.

There are countless times I have witnessed physical health complaints clearing up once someone has been able to express how they are feeling more easily, so this is an added bonus.

Don't stew

A fter talking about what a great thing it is to express yourself, here's the curve ball; don't bottle up emotions but also **don't stew**. During sessions with the majority of my clients, I have found that they only need to express their feelings about a key or core problem once or twice as 'the cleanse' to make them feel better. They feel a sense of relief once their emotions have been expressed and this is a good sign of progress.

But what happens if we keep talking about the same problem? It begins to not feel good again. If we keep talking about the same thing over and over again we can begin to feel worse. This is because we are stewing over our problems rather than resolving them and moving forwards. Stewing takes us down The Happiness Barometer.

Don't stew, you will feel worse if you do

Learn to listen to how you are feeling when you talk about a particular topic or problem. If you feel better when or just after you express your feelings then it is probably still beneficial to talk about it.

If however you begin to feel worse, then this is a good indicator that you have talked about it enough and need a new perspective.

Think back to the example of the child banging into the table. The child was hurt, but he expressed himself, which rebalanced him. He then moved on, back to playing, laughing and running about. He did not keep talking about it. He did not go over the accident and analyse why the table was there, who bought it, why it was that height, whether a parent had placed it there, thereby making it their fault. It is very common for people to blame their parents for most things by the way! The point is, a child doesn't naturally stew on problems and nor should we.

From stewing to success

Let me give you an example relating to one of my clients. This was a lady in her early twenties who had a problem with cystitis (a bladder inflammation) and who was generally feeling very low. She told me that she was very worried about the relationship between her mother and father. They weren't getting on, and she thought a lot about what would happen if they were to split up, and whether her Mum would cope. She hadn't told anyone about this fear.

During our first session we talked about how she felt about her Mum and Dad's situation, as that was the most prominent thing on her mind.

At our second session she reported she was beginning to feel better. She had started expressing these fears and worries to me, so was beginning to feel happier. She continued to talk more about her parents.

By the time we got to her third session, she said she was feeling quite a bit better. She then started to talk about her Mum and Dad again. This time when she spoke about them, I sensed a different feeling about the topic. Instead of it being a cleanse, it felt like we were going over old ground for the sake of it. I stopped her to ask how it felt to talk about them again, and she admitted it did not feel great.

After the initial relief and benefit of letting out what she had been holding onto, she was now simply stewing about the situation and it wasn't doing her any good. I needed to get her back to focusing on herself again.

I suggested that we change the subject and asked her to tell me what she wanted to do with her life. She paused, gathering her thoughts for a moment. She had been so fixated on her Mum and Dad's story that it had taken up most of her headspace. She therefore found it hard to just let go of it but she agreed to try. Up until that point she had dropped out of university and was just hanging around at home.

We continued to work together for a few more weeks to help her feel better in herself. By the time our sixth session arrived she positively bounced in, excited to tell me about the new ideas and creative projects she was planning. She had contacted a different university and made the decision to apply there. When I asked her out of interest about her parents, as they had been the biggest cause of stress for her just six weeks earlier, she said, "Oh they're fine, to be honest I haven't given them a second thought!".

This is a great example of how, when we move ourselves up The Happiness Barometer, our ideas change and stresses decrease. Problems can simply dissolve, not by them necessarily going away, but by having a new perspective on them. The better we feel, the better our lives will be. We will see things in a whole new way.

When we learn to avoid stewing on our problems, we take a big step forward in our quest to feel good

My rule of thumb is that if a topic does not feel good, don't talk about it more than once or twice. When we stew we become trapped and powerless, and as we know by now, life should be a lot more fun than that.

Let others off the hook

A ll too often when I meet with a client for the first time, within the first few sentences, or first few words even, they will recount a tale about how they have been wronged, mistreated or upset by someone.

Now here's the thing. Is your state of mind really down to someone else? Do they really make you feel a certain way, or are you simply reacting in a certain way to them?

In our quest to move up The Happiness Barometer, seeing someone as directly responsible for how we are feeling is a no-no.

Ultimately the choice is ours to either blame others **or** focus on feeling better ourselves. Holding onto someone or something that has negatively affected you is a big mind and energy drain. Don't give your power away to them. It is vital to realise that we are worth so much more than that.

Free yourself, let them off the hook, and move on

Even if we only make small changes, by focusing on what truly makes us happy and recognising that we are in charge of our own happiness, we will become happier. This process is not always easy but the more we practice, the more we can let others be.

Letting someone else off the hook is liberating.

With this new found emotional freedom, up The Happiness Barometer we go!

Stop resisting

A few years ago I found myself spending some time with a modern day monk called Sandy C Newbigging. He asked me about my life and background, and I found myself telling him that my Dad and I had been estranged for 15 years, which was a painful, frustrating and ongoing situation. We had parted ways for a variety of complicated reasons and had been unable to resolve our differences. I went into great detail about the sequence of events that led to the point where we didn't see each other, placing the blame at the feet of various people and circumstances that I believed had caused the rift. I said that if the situation had been different 15 years ago, then things would be different now and I would be a happier person.

After this long and protracted story he looked at me and said, "You are resisting your past".

"Resisting it?" I thought indignantly, "What do you mean? I'm not resisting it, I've just spent the last 20 minutes giving you all the ins and outs of the situation!"

He replied, "You are resisting it, and not letting it go. Let it be and you will reduce your own suffering."

At last the penny dropped. I had to let go of how it had been. Life is as it is.

Blaming, shaming and wanting things to be different to how they actually were, was not going to change what had happened, and continually dwelling on it was actually making me feel worse. It was like I was 'freeze-framing' that point in my life and getting stuck there.

Was my state of mind now dependent on what happened 15 years ago? Only if I allowed it to be.

I realised that I can create a new and different way. I can create a way that means I focus on what makes me happy now and who I have around me now. The past, no matter how painful or upsetting, doesn't have to affect who I am today. As I began to feel better and better in myself, I found that I wasn't as charged, annoyed or frustrated about the situation. I could think about it in a whole new way.

What I realised was that I had the power to move forwards. I could choose to focus on what makes me feel good, on my work, my wife, my children, my family, my friends and the wonderful life that I wanted to create.

Empowering ourselves to stop dwelling and start living in the here and now makes all the difference

Go for what you want

If you are not feeling great try asking yourself this question…

What do I really want?

As we have already seen there are a few reasons for unhappiness, but this simple question is capable of getting to the root of many problems.

Not going for what we really want, or know we are capable of, is arguably the most common reason why people are unhappy. When we deny or block what we want, unhappiness is often the end result.

This concept is covered in greater detail in 'Way 7 – Pimp up your purpose', but it is worth noting here that our emotions are intrinsically linked to respond best when we are doing what we love. The creation of that buzz and internal excitement by going for what we really want, will certainly take us up The Happiness Barometer.

The thought of actually getting where we want to be in life is a very satisfying and exciting vision. If this vision is right for us, then the accompanying excitement will give us the energy to get there. It is a part of expressing who we are and what we were put on earth to do.

Do what you love

The principle of 'Doing what you love' seems so simple, but for some reason many people really struggle to achieve it. We can find ourselves making excuse after excuse: responsibilities, bills, low energy, no time. These are all valid reasons but Rome wasn't built in a day. We are all capable of taking small steps towards a goal, which one day may enable us to do what we love full-time.

In the meantime, creating time in our day for things that we enjoy and are passionate about can only take us up The Happiness Barometer. It could be taking dancing lessons, reading a thrilling novel or taking an evening stroll; whatever gives us a chance to do something that we love. The key is that only you can put these things into your day. Stop waiting for them to happen, or waiting for others to create the opportunities and just go for it! Creating internal stories about how things will change in days, months or years, is only putting off the happiness that we could be having right now.

Often people are so busy living that they forget to do what they love, what brings them joy, pleasure and fun. A 'To Do' list without anything fun on it will soon become a 'To Don't' list. To get up The

Happiness Barometer it is crucial to add things into our days or weeks that we love.

So make a list of the things you love doing, pin it on the fridge door and start doing something towards achieving them right away.

Make time for fun, not excuses

WAY 3
Tend your emotional garden

·BAROMETER RISING TIPS·

Nurture your positive emotions

Don't bottle things up

Don't stew over and dwell on negative situations

Let others be, your happiness is not dependant on them

Stop resisting life but instead allow it to be as it is

Go for what you want

Do more of what you love

Jump on The Groovy Train of Thought

WAY 4

Filling your head with the good stuff

E very day we have thousands of thoughts running through our heads, and supposedly a very large proportion of these are typically negative, which is a fairly sad statistic. For many years I have been working out how to think better, happier and more positively rather than allowing stressful, draining and limiting thoughts to dominate.

Every aspect of our lives, minute to minute, hour to hour, day to day is influenced by how we think. The quality of our thoughts impacts our work, our home life and our relationships. They also significantly influence our choices, our conversations, our outlook and even our health, especially if we allow stressful thoughts to linger too long.

Thoughts set the scene in life, so it is crucial to be aware of this, and to consciously manage them if we can.

We are in an era where so much emphasis is put on our physical health, we are constantly told about new diets, eating regimes and how best to exercise. Eating well and exercise are both very important, but how come such little attention is devoted to the way we think and feel?

It is hard to function well in life when we continually have stressful, unhappy or draining thoughts. Life becomes tedious and plain annoying, all happiness drains away. In this state our headspace is at the mercy of our thoughts, which can lead to mood swings or even depression. Surely there is a way to make it the other way around?

How would life be if we could decide to make our thoughts good instead of bad?

If they could work in our favour, making us feel good, enhancing our life and the way we see things. Can we say goodbye to the negative stream of chatter in our heads? I used to wonder if this was actually possible. What I have discovered over the years, is that not only is it possible, but with a bit of practice anyone can do it.

I used to believe that the only way to do this would involve becoming some sort of Zen master, living at the top of a very high mountain in a mud hut, far removed from the rat race, spending every waking moment concentrating on clearing my mind and focusing on inner peace.

The good news is, thankfully we don't have to go to such extremes. It is much easier to control our own thoughts by simply learning some of the rules which govern them.

Having good thoughts can really change our lives, improving how we deal with problems and positively shaping our futures, which in turn makes life feel so much better, freer and easier.

The obvious question is how do we make this important change? Where are these good thoughts? How do we get them into our lives, and more importantly our heads? What needs to happen to get our thoughts working for us and not against us?

There are a number of techniques which I recommend to my clients to improve their thinking. They require lots of practice, but once we can get the hang of a new way of thinking, the improvements will be dramatic and up The Happiness Barometer we will go.

Bye bye bingo ball brain

H ave you ever noticed that there are times when there is no rhyme or reason to your thoughts? They bounce around like bingo balls in the bingo machine of your brain, before popping out in a sequence of their choice. Ideas, problems, situations, stresses, plans, fun times, sad times, things to sort out, inner dialogue, shopping lists, partners, ex-partners, worries, memories… the list is endless.

This exercise is about becoming much more conscious and in control of your thoughts. Instead of just letting them pop out at random, like balls in a bingo ball machine, you can start to become more aware of how they are feeling as they arrive.

Just take a moment now to let some thoughts flow through your mind. Consider different ideas and situations, people, friends, family, anything that pops into your head. Notice how you feel as the thoughts arrive, which thoughts make you happy, sad, excited, annoyed, indifferent, despondent? A whole spectrum of thoughts and topics pass through our minds, (and we will get on to why they either feel good or bad shortly), but for now just be aware that they usually fall into one of two categories:

• Good-feeling thoughts
• Negative-feeling thoughts

This is a simple but crucial point. Good-feeling thoughts help you feel happy, bad-feeling thoughts do not.

Realise that your thoughts have feelings too

Becoming aware of how thoughts feel as they arrive in our minds is the first crucial step in being able to make our minds happier. Only when we are able to recognise the difference can we take charge of our thoughts, rather than letting the thoughts take charge of us.

As a good thought creates a good-feeling, we want to fill our heads with as many of these as possible, because they will raise us up The Happiness Barometer, with all the benefits we have seen so far. Obviously bad-feeling thoughts have the reverse effect and take us down. We don't want bad-feeling thoughts to influence our life. To improve our overall happiness, the key is to flood our heads and lives with good-feeling thoughts.

Thoughts have momentum

If the first step was to realise that thoughts carry a feeling, then the second step would be to realise that each thought creates a momentum.

Have you ever noticed that when you are in a bad mood, within a few moments your thoughts have gathered pace, grouping together in your mind, creating a really negative stew in your head?

If you hold a particular thought in your head for a small period of time, even just a few seconds, then frequently another thought of the same type will appear and join it. Your thoughts will link up like a set of train carriages, with one type of thought linking to another one which has a similar feeling.

Conversely when you are in a good mood, thinking good thoughts, these too will link together, creating a positive and happy stream of thoughts.

Our thoughts have their own momentum and they will carry on in the manner in which they start, unless we can either stop or change them.

Negative thoughts link to
other negative thoughts

Positive thoughts create more
positive thoughts

The Groovy Train
versus
The Negative Train

With this said it is now time to take charge and decide which train of thought you want to aim for. It's time to jump on a locomotive.

The Groovy Train of Thought

On The Groovy Train our thoughts are happy, exciting, empowering, freeing and clear, which makes us feel as if we can jump over life's hurdles. It feels good to be on The Groovy Train, a happy life comes from a happy train of thoughts.

94

The Negative Train of Thought

The Negative Train is just the opposite, it is a stressful, unhappy, annoying and irritating train to be on. These thoughts are negative, sad, powerless, depressing, helpless and pessimistic.

Let's look at an example of how this works. Imagine a scenario where you are wondering why a good friend hasn't phoned you for a while?

The Negative Train

On this train you will be thinking…

'I knew she wouldn't phone me… and my sister hasn't bothered to call either… and I didn't get invited over to her house last week… I bet other people did… probably because she doesn't like me very much… and she went away without me for New Year… I bet she had a better time without me there…'

The Negative Train now has a whole load of negative carriages linking up, which started with the first negative-feeling thought.

The destination for this kind of train is usually straight to a pity party for one. This train will even get there on automatic pilot if you let it. It is really important to avoid this kind of train as it will do nothing but make you feel worse. The pity party is not a fun place to be at all!

The Groovy Train

In the same scenario, let's see what you will be thinking if you have jumped on The Groovy Train instead and start with better-feeling thoughts about the situation:

'I hope she is ok… I bet she is busy… I hope she's enjoying what she's up to… it was so great to see her last time we met up…. we had such a laugh together… I'm really looking forward to hearing from her when we both have a bit more time…'

As you can see, The Groovy Train creates a good feeling inside. The sequence of thoughts runs smoothly and creates a pleasant happy feeling in our heads. These good-feeling thoughts make us feel more content and calm, they also give us clarity enabling us to see the best way to do things.

Our job is to become much more aware of how our thoughts are feeling as soon as we think them, because they create a momentum that we either want (The Groovy Train) or we don't want (The Negative Train).

Jumping on
The Groovy Train

Y ou may be thinking at this stage, how can I get myself onto The Groovy Train more often? Let's take a look at some ways to do this.

Hammer it away

An exercise which I suggest my clients use to try to improve their thoughts is the concept of 'Hammer it away'. This involves a bit of fun mental imagery. Think of the game at fun fairs where moles pop up randomly out of their holes and you have to hammer them down with the mallet. Well the same principle can be applied to unpleasant thoughts (using the mental image if that helps). Simply hammer away the ones that don't feel great, refusing to entertain them at all.

If it doesn't feel good, say "no thanks" to the negative thought and hammer it away

This process becomes easier the more you practice it. It is really helpful in making us aware and conscious of our thoughts. It enables us to allow the thoughts that feel good in, and hammer away the ones that don't, literally without giving them a second thought.

Thought pick 'n' mix

Do you remember how exciting it was to go to the Pick 'n' Mix section in the sweet shop as a child? You had your empty bag ready and there before you were hundreds of sweets and treats to choose from. You could chose all the ones you wanted the most: the ones that made your tongue tingle; sweet or sour; chocolate or jelly; choosing all these favourites made you feel good. If you ended up with a sweet you didn't like, you simply didn't choose it the next time around.

What I'm saying here is that we can do the same with our thoughts. We need to choose them wisely, because the good ones make us feel good, but we have to avoid going back to the ones that make us feel bad.

The more thoughts we can choose that feel good, the more Groovy Trains we can get on. The Negative Train, with its carriages full of negativity, should be avoided as often as possible.

Power of direct focus

How we focus our minds is a seriously powerful choice that we make every day. In my experience, the more I focus on a topic, situation or problem, the bigger it becomes in my mind. This works both ways; great ideas and happy things can flourish and grow, but focusing on negative ideas and issues can send us off in the wrong direction. We can get ourselves really wound up by focusing on situations that don't feel good, so let's stop doing it!

What you focus on gets bigger and bigger, just like a snowball

The trick is to focus on anything that feels a bit better. Think about happy memories, somebody who inspires you, things that make you laugh, your love of nature, your life goals, what you enjoy about your job, your best friend… the list is endless. Use your imagination if you have to, this is what kids do brilliantly! Thinking about anything that creates better-feeling thoughts will work, this will get you on board The Groovy Train.

Choose topics, ideas, plans or times in your life that feel good to you

You are in charge of your focus so start focusing well, snowball your thoughts in the right direction, you will feel better when you do. Focusing on positive things will take you up The Happiness Barometer.

Rope swing action

What happens if you are only able to have one or two consecutive good thoughts, before other more negative things come to mind? Well, another helpful technique which many of my clients find useful is to practice the art of 'Rope swing action'.

Did you ever go across a stream on a rope swing when you were a child? If you did, can you remember how tightly you had to hold on to it, until it took you to the other side? You can use the same technique to hold onto good thoughts. In your mind hold on to the good thought as long as you possibly can, allowing it to swing you over to the next one. If you fall off, find another thought that feels better and try holding on to that one. It is your positive focus that is important here.

Even if you only have one or two subjects that make you feel happy, something as simple as how much you love your cat, or how you admire your favourite football team, reading or playing the guitar, whatever gives you a strong happy thought, stick with it. If you can hold onto it the chances are it will begin to multiply. If your mind wanders off into negative thoughts, recognise that they don't feel good and bring your mind back to something that gets you back on The Groovy Train.

Become a mind bouncer

A few years ago, I got talking to a man who owned a night club. He explained that it cost him a lot of money to have bouncers on the door every night, and sometimes he wondered if he needed to keep them on, especially as there hadn't been any trouble in his club for a while. The truth is that there was probably less trouble at the club because the bouncers were there. They were stopping people who they believed might ruin the atmosphere in the club. They were also stopping the club from getting too full, because if it become too full, then no-one could enjoy it.

This got me thinking about how overcrowded our minds can become, and that we are in need of mind bouncers.

Imagine that our mind bouncers are in charge of both the quality and quantity of our thoughts. They choose which thoughts to let in to create the best atmosphere, and they control the number of thoughts zooming in and out of our heads too.

Life today is full of so many different inputs coming at us constantly via social media, newspapers, TV and radio and via phones, email and online, both locally and globally. We are bombarded with information all day and night, and unfortunately more often than not, the media seems to prefer focusing on the sad or depressing stories.

When I went to visit a client at his home recently, the first thing I noticed was that he had a huge TV screen in his lounge showing News 24. He said that he kept it on twenty four hours a day, as it kept him company. Unsurprisingly he was depressed. If you are hanging out at the bottom of The Happiness Barometer, you can become obsessed with negative ideas and stories, which perpetuate and exacerbate your fragile mental state.

Too much negativity will almost certainly influence how we feel, it can become overwhelming and this will take us down The Happiness Barometer. This is where I suggest your mind bouncer can play a part.

I advised my client to turn off the constant news. I proposed that he limit himself to one news show a day, or preferably one a week, stopping its constant presence in his life. He agreed to turn it off. He soon realised how much it had been influencing his mood, as he absorbed the constant negativity all day long.

You may not have noticed just how much bad news can drain the life force out of you. It plays on our minds, influencing how we feel. Now that I am aware of the dangers of too much negativity,

I sometimes go cold turkey and have a news detox, with four or five days away from any news input.

This is harder than you would imagine thanks to TV, radio, computers and phones firing it constantly, but well worth trying if possible. I believe that people can significantly improve their mood by just not watching the news. It is time to get picky, make some conscious choices about what you allow in your mind and create your own mind bouncer.

The same principle applies to idle gossip and negative conversations. We need to stop stockpiling negativity, because it does no-one any favours.

As we move up The Happiness Barometer, we find that we have less time for negativity, preferring instead to aim for a happier mental place. We learn to see the best in people and situations, rather than focusing on their more negative aspects. The seeds of negativity should have no place to flourish in our minds.

Only allow in to your head what suits you and what feels good to you, this will make a world of difference

Getting on at the right station

I've found that when you are not feeling good hanging out towards the bottom of The Happiness Barometer, just thinking positive is not very easy; sometimes it feels downright impossible. To start a Groovy Train of Thought it is important to get on at the right station to begin with.

Here are some other tips to improve your thinking when you are struggling:

Walk away from the tangled net

Have you ever been so caught up in negative thinking that you can't see any way out of it? You are so tangled up in the situation or problem, that negative trains of thought are running wild, and the more you try to fix the problem, the more tangled you seem to get in its net?

It can be tricky to change your thinking when you are completely tangled up in a messy situation in your mind. My advice is simple, stop the struggle, lift off the net and walk away from it. Then do something completely different.

If you put the problem down, you can go and do something else that helps you feel better, then you can either come back to it or not, depending on how you feel.

The benefit of this is, as you feel better your thoughts will become better, so you will see solutions more easily. When you are tangled up, it is a negative perspective that you are seeing and believing. When you are higher up The Happiness Barometer it is easier to think more clearly.

Do things you love

Doing things you love will create a good feeling inside. This good feeling moves you up The Happiness Barometer and will lead to better thinking.

Make a list of things which will pick you up and make sure you start to do them. Here are some activities that people have said helped them quickly feel better and move away from problems in their mind…

• Exercising
• Watching comedy
• Phoning a good friend
• Listening to uplifting music
• Gardening
• Yoga
• Dancing

There are hundreds more but you get the idea.

Try to think of a few things that might help pick you up. Find things that will quickly and easily improve your mindset and mood. These must be things you can do which are not reliant on others; the aim is to empower your own good mood now. Waiting until a week on Friday, when a friend can go with you to the cinema, is not what we are after here. Sure, aim to do that as well, but these are supposed to be small and easily achievable instant mood lifters.

This method takes us out of our Negative Train of Thought, and makes us actively do something to help ourselves feel a bit better. It is much easier to find a solution to a problem when you are feeling good in yourself, than trying to do so when your mind is in a tangle.

It is also worth noting that it is never a good idea to start an argument when your head is in a tangled net! Bad mood arguments rarely have good outcomes. Try to get into a better-feeling place first and decide if you still need to have that discussion. So many times people realise with regret what they have said following an argument, very often a tangled net can be blamed for clouding their judgement.

With practice you will realise that the best way to solve a problem is to step away from the tangled net, and instead do something that improves your mindset, later you can look for a solution. This tends to have far better results.

Staying on The Groovy Train

Have you ever noticed how the same situation can look and feel different with a new perspective? Changing our thinking whilst in the midst of a situation can help.

Recently I was on a very busy train leaving London, it was jam-packed, nose to nose, and I had to stand all the way to my station in a tight, airless carriage. At first my thinking was negative, after a long day I was tired, so the complaints began mounting up in my head. I was focusing entirely on what was wrong with the situation: trains are too small these days; there are too many people commuting; perhaps I will stop commuting altogether and only work from home; why does that man not use deodorant, etc!

The negative thoughts were flowing fast so unsurprisingly this was making me feel terrible.

Instead of allowing my negative thoughts to control me, I took some slow deep breaths. I got rid of the thoughts that didn't feel good and searched my mind for better ones.

I changed my focus and I looked for a Groovy Train to board in my head

My first thought was to take some deep breaths and appreciate what a gift it is to actually be breathing. I felt wonder at how oxygen travels around my body to every cell allowing me to stay alive. Next I thought about a night out that was coming up with some old school friends who I have known for over thirty years, I started remembering some funny times we had had together at school, and chuckled to myself.

Then I looked at the man and women who were sitting straight in front of me, leaning in to each other, and I wondered how long they had been a couple. Next I began thinking about where we might take our children for a fun day out, and how excited they would be when we told them. The good thoughts were now flowing fast, taking me out of my physical discomfort and off to a much happier place in my mind.

I created a state of mind that felt better by changing what I was thinking about. By staying on The Groovy Train with my thoughts, the same situation became better.

Don't compare yourself to others

Theodore Roosevelt once said "Comparison is the thief of joy". Comparing yourself to others and feeling jealous is such a negative trap to fall into. It somehow gives you the feeling that you can't create your own brilliant life. Get inspired by what others are up to yes, let them motivate you even, but more importantly get excited by your own potential and plans, because they are the plans that matter.

Find the best in someone

Think about someone you like being around or who inspires you, what are their qualities? This can help you feel better and motivate you. When it comes to people who annoy you, if you can't avoid them, then try to find the best in them instead. Everyone has some good qualities, so look for the positives and focus on them. If you concentrate on someone else's negative aspects, it will only bring you down The Happiness Barometer, not them, so it is a waste of energy. Learning to see the best in other people helps us to think better ourselves and stay on The Groovy Train.

Focus on the best outcome

If you find that you are worrying about a friend or family member, work out in your mind what the best outcome for them could be in their current situation. This outcome may or may not happen, but remember that you are not in charge of their life, it is up to them. Your job is to create a better-feeling place in yourself, so thinking about the best outcome for them may help you feel better. You may or may not choose to help them, but if you decide to try, then your involvement should feel more positive, because it is coming from this better-feeling place.

Laugh at yourself or anything else

Comedy is a great way to feel better, we all enjoy a good laugh. I find comedians or amusing clips on TV or Youtube help me to relax and feel good. Even if I am cooking dinner I will put something funny on in the background to help nurture my good mood. Even laughing at myself (if I find myself in a difficult situation) can improve how I feel. Have a try, your mind may just thank you for it. If it works then keep doing it, whether it is comedy, music, radio chat, or whatever. It is easy to change your perspective once you find a way that feels better to you.

Your life will change

C reating better thoughts is a bit of an art-form and can be fun once you get the hang of it.

I believe negative thoughts aren't just there for the sake of being difficult. If our thoughts feel bad it is because we are thinking about something in the wrong way and our perspective needs to change. Conversely if our thoughts feel good it is because we must be thinking about something in the right way.

If we allow The Negative Train to take over we will feel drained, sad and demotivated. Believing that we can't achieve something, thinking badly about others, all of these negative thoughts go against the grain of who we are as human beings. Self doubt, loathing and criticism never feel any good.

On the other hand, when we have good thoughts we feel energised and excited. Better empowered, more loving thoughts will link together and can change our perspective on almost everything if we allow them to. Training ourselves to think positively in this way, as often as possible, will have a hugely beneficial impact on our emotional health.

I now work with my thoughts and enjoy them as part of the feedback system in my life. If I am thinking badly, I know that it is because there must be a better way to think about something or that my perspective is off. I now know that I need to find a way to move up The Happiness Barometer by improving how I am thinking.

If we can create better ways of thinking this will certainly make our lives more enjoyable and empowering. It is our job to consciously decide to work our way up The Happiness Barometer, because life is so much better towards the top.

The techniques we have covered in this chapter will take some practice, but with a little effort a great outcome is totally achievable.

You can change what you are thinking about so take charge of your mind and happiness, and fill your head with the good stuff!

My happy thoughts list

. . . .

. . . .

. . . .

. . . .

. . . .

. . . .

My happy things to focus on

. . . .

. . . .

. . . .

. . . .

. . . .

. . . .

WAY 4
Jump on The Groovy Train of Thought

· BAROMETER RISING TIPS ·

Jump on Groovy Trains of Thought that feel good

Hammer away negative thoughts

Good thoughts link to other good thoughts

Focus on topics that make you feel better

Be your own mind bouncer and only allow positive things in

Listen to your wise old gut

WAY 5

Our instinct is a powerful tool

There is someone who knows you very well, better than anyone else and sometimes, better than you know yourself. They always know what is right for you and they do their best to let you know. Even when you may not be listening.

Who is this all-seeing and all-knowing person? It's you of course!

We are all familiar with phrases like 'listen to your gut', 'gut feeling', and having a 'gut instinct'. They are terms for our own powerful 'knowing' that comes from within. Knowing what is right for us and knowing which direction to take in our lives.

Our instinct knows best and is one of the most powerful tools in the toolbox of our lives. Instinct rules supreme, and without it we can find ourselves directionless in life, drifting like a rudderless boat on an ocean, with no land in sight.

Instinct is the strongest and most reliable guidance

system we have. We just have to learn to listen to it and then learn how to act on it.

The clever thing is that our wise old gut somehow knows what is best for us even before we do. It is an inner sense, a kind of knowing that sits within us. Always listen to this inner voice, it is connected to who we are and knows what is right for us.

Our wise old guts guide us through both the big and small choices in life. Through the tricky and the good times. This instinct helps us make good decisions in so many ways regarding relationships, career choices and our life direction. It also guides small everyday choices, for example deciding which is the best seat to choose in the pub, where to walk on a Sunday afternoon, or deciding which people you are going to speak to at a party. It seems trivial but if you think about it, it's true. It's all guided for us if we would just listen!

Decisions or choices which didn't feel right in our gut, seem to invariably fail or be difficult. Have you ever found this?

Practice listening to your instincts and notice how life changes when you begin to tune in and act accordingly.

Not listening creates a bumpy ride

I have seen hundreds of people in my clinic over the years who, when looking back over their lives and recalling a particular situation, say that before they made that decision, they knew somewhere deep inside themselves that it wasn't right, but that they went ahead regardless. They ignored their own inner sense of what was right for them, and instead took more notice of other factors such as logic, fear, other people's opinions or their own insecurities.

Here are a couple of common examples...

"I knew I shouldn't have taken that job, it didn't feel right when I took it and surprise surprise it didn't work out."

"I knew on day one when I started this relationship, even on my wedding day, that it wasn't right. I should have trusted my instincts."

When we go against what we know is right for us, it often seems to create a bumpy ride, which means that life after this decision doesn't flow very well.

One of the questions I always ask my clients who are pondering a big decision in their life is, "What does your instinct tell you?"

This is a great way of getting someone to really think about, and listen to, what they know is right and conversely not right, for them.

One useful rule of thumb is that instinct creates a calm and peaceful feeling, along with a sense of inner rightness, which is felt from our core. It is quite difficult to sum up in words, but we all know how it feels. If we are feeling panicky or anxious when making a decision then it is unlikely that we are following our instincts, it is far more likely that we are listening to our fears and anxieties instead.

Instinct is a sense before thinking

So how do we tune in to our wise old guts?

My advice is first try to relax and then listen in.
If you are really having trouble knowing what your
instinct is telling you on any given topic, then find
a place of relaxation and a way to feel relaxed.
This may be having a hot bath, walking in the park,
enjoying a bike ride or getting out into nature.
Wherever enables you to get rid of some of the
'internal noise' in your head and listen in to your
true self, by which I mean the calm and knowing
wise person inside us all.

Take some slow deep breaths. Slow breathing
can help to create a peaceful and relaxed state.
Then ask yourself the question that needs to be
answered, then listen and feel what your inner
guidance is telling you.

Chances are the answer won't come from your
head, don't try to think about the question even,
the answer should come from your gut.

The calmer you are the easier it will be to tune
in. The guidance provided by our wise old gut is
always there, it never switches off. Our increasingly
busy lives sometimes make it difficult to sense
what it's telling us, but I guarantee with practice
and time, you will be able to hear your own inner
voice.

Sometimes people ignore their instincts, mainly because they are set on a particular path in life, or believe that paying proper attention to what their gut is telling them will send them off in a direction in which they don't want to travel. Maybe they want to get out of a relationship but don't know how, or perhaps they don't want to let down a loved one or rock the boat too much.

The more uncomfortable we feel about a particular situation, the more our gut is trying to tell us that it is not right, or that something needs to change.

Listen to your inner voice

This is another reason why some people can end up feeling low or depressed, they are not listening to their inner guidance, they are not acting on it and subsequently they can't avoid feeling low. If we are not listening to what is right for us, inevitably we will sink down The Happiness Barometer.

However, as we learn to trust and use this powerful instinctive tool we will see dramatic life changes, either in the big things like work and relationships, or simply in achieving a long-held goal; we can use our wise old guts to feel our way there.

Our wise old guts are directly linked to who we are, so listening to our instincts will always take us higher up The Happiness Barometer.

Playing the hot and cold game

If you want to practice using your instincts, think about the game 'Hot and Cold'. I used to play this as a child with my brother Rob. One of us would hide an object in the house or garden, then the other would have to find it by being directed towards it, with the call of "Warmer" meaning you were moving towards the object or "Colder" if you were moving away. When one was virtually on top of the object, the other would shout, "Hot! Hot!".

This game strategy can also be applied to life... try it. Listen to whether you feel 'hot' or 'cold' about a situation, idea, person or purchase which you are considering. If your instinct is positive, then you should move towards it exploring further. If your instincts are negative, they are telling you not to take things any further.

The more you can tune into what feels positive and good, and move towards it, the better your life will become.

Relief is an indicator

A nother way to tune into an instinct is through a sense of relief when a decision is made. It is the flip side of the instinctive coin as it were. If we feel a sense of relief after making a difficult or negative choice then the chances are that what we were about to do or embark upon, probably wasn't right for us in the first place. Again, here are a few common examples…

Q. "How did you feel when you broke up with your fiancé?"

A. "Relief because I knew the relationship wasn't right."

Q. "How did you feel abort not taking that job in another city?"

A. "Relief, as I knew it wasn't right for me to leave my family."

Q. "How did you feel when you decided not to take up that course?"

A. "Relief, as I realised it was too much to take on with small children."

I find that if a decision is right, then what follows generally runs smoothly, and gives us a surge of energy and excitement.

If the decision wasn't right for us, and we decide to not go for something which felt wrong, then this is often followed by a sense of relief. Whatever it was probably wasn't right for you or perhaps it just wasn't the right time for you.
Ask yourself…

Would I feel relieved if it didn't happen?

The answer to this question can help guide you more clearly. It is about finding a way to make things work out as well as possible by listening to your gut.

Unblocking the dam to a better life

I would like to share another client case study to round off this chapter about following our wise old guts.

A lady in her late thirties got in touch asking for my help because her life was in a bit of a mess. She was anxious, feeling lost and full of doubts. She had numerous physical symptoms and wasn't sleeping well. She was basically at her wits' end.

126

Her children were eight and ten years old and although she loved being a mum, and all the joys and trials that go with it, still she knew something important was missing in her life. She was merely going through the motions, doing the chores, making sure her family were ok, but a huge part of her was deeply unhappy.

I asked her what gives her a buzz and what her instinct was telling her.

She said that she longed for her old career, the socialising and creativity. She used to work in marketing and she had loved everything about it; the vibe, her colleagues, the constant challenges and excitement. I could see by how her eyes lit up when she talked that we were onto something.

I asked her again what her instinct was telling her?

"I would love to do some similar work now", she said, eyes lighting up again, "BUT I can't. It probably won't work. I'm too old now..." and here followed a physical slump.

"What a great nonsense belief!" I said.

I'm not always that direct with my clients, but I wanted my words to have an impact. She knew what her instinct was telling her but was talking herself out of it. She sat there slightly shocked at what I had said, and with a thoughtful face asked, "What do you mean by 'nonsense belief'?"

"Well, you have created a belief that is nonsense! You are only thirty-seven years old and you love doing this kind of work. Why can't you go and find some?"

A wave of realisation came over her face. She began to accept that this could be a possibility and I saw her visibly light up again.

The issue was clear. She had focused on what was wrong with her life, and how she was failing to move forwards (both of which are surefire ways to make you feel bad) and as a result her state of mind had just got worse and worse. As she slipped down the rungs of The Happiness Barometer, refusing to acknowledge or listen to her instincts which were telling her to get back to the work she loved, her beliefs and ideas spiralled further into negativity, hence the anxieties and negative thoughts.

A few weeks later she called to say that she was feeling fantastic! She had been researching marketing agencies, applying for jobs and was very excited about the future.

She had unblocked the dam that was holding her life back!

If we stop ourselves going for what we want, just like damming a river, we create an emotional backlog of feelings such as frustration, worry and misery.

The more we refuse to go with our instincts the worse we will feel.

Once we realise this and trust what feels right, our dams will unblock and we will start flowing in the direction that feels right to us. Our energy, motivation, confidence and excitement will all come back.

Following our wise old gut prevents damming the flow of our lives and instead opens doors of opportunity

Our wise old gut knows best, we must listen to it to find life-changing happiness.

WAY 5
Listen to your wise old gut

· BAROMETER RISING TIPS ·

Trust your gut and what
it is telling you

Your instinct rules supreme,
it is your guidance system

Remember relief is an
indication that something
wasn't right

Listen to what feels right
and follow it!

Turn your 'muck' to luck

WAY 6

Bouncing back

S tuff happens in life, that's a given. Sometimes small niggling stuff, sometimes big life-changing stuff. Either way, whatever is going on, finding a way to be able to move forward and see things with clarity, is the key to unlocking the door to our life-changing happiness.

Feeling we have been knocked in life can take us dipping towards the bottom of The Happiness Barometer with stressful and negative thoughts. It is crucial to do whatever it takes to help ourselves get back up towards the top again, so we can overcome situations from the best place possible.

Remember the Weebles? The toy which, however it got pushed over, always stood straight back up again. The same goes for us, the more we can learn to self-right ourselves automatically, the stronger and more resilient we become. Some knocks are more difficult to take than others, but knowing it is possible is the first step.

Whether we are feeling stuck in a rut or are knee-deep in some tricky life situations, being able to respond and react in an empowering way with a positive perspective is what makes all the difference. When we do, up The Happiness Barometer we go.

Roll with it

D o things ever happen that you know don't have to annoy you, but they just do? Running for but just missing a bus, getting stuck in a traffic jam, a train home being delayed or someone cancelling a night out at the last minute are some examples. When this type of situation arises you have a choice, ask yourself…

Can I do anything about this?

Is it worth me getting into a bad mood about it?

Does it need to affect my happiness in a negative way?

If we let a situation negatively get to us this can quickly take us sliding down The Happiness Barometer. We can obviously pick ourselves up again from here, but it is far easier not to fall down in the first place if possible.

Making a choice to just 'Roll with it' is the answer. The above may sound like small examples, but if we frequently react negatively to these type of situations the cumulative effect can ruin our whole day.

Roll with it plus

To take this one step further how about trying to turn these situations from something negative into something positive instead? For example…

Missed the bus?

Try striking up an interesting conversation at the bus stop

Stuck in traffic?

At least that means more time to listen to your favourite radio station in the car

Delayed train?

Organise your diary and spend time thinking about all the great plans you have coming up

Cancelled night out?

Go to see a movie you have been dying to see or call an old friend and go out with them instead

By rolling with it (or rolling with it plus) we can remain in a better-feeling place. By not allowing circumstances to dictate our mood we don't allow ourselves to be taken down The Happiness Barometer.

The super trooper mindset

M eet Super Trooper and Drooper; they see life
  very differently.

Super Trooper has a mindset that sees the best in
things, stays upbeat and is set on feeling good.
Drooper has a mindset that sees things in a
negative or difficult way and basically has trouble
feeling anything but bad.

It is so important to see the distinction between
the two, and how a change of perspective can
improve everything. Life will throw all sorts of things
at us but it is the mindset we adopt which helps us
to feel differently about the challenges we face.

We have the choice to see things in a better way. Let's take a look at the Drooper versus the Super Trooper mentality:

Drooper	Super Trooper
Blames circumstances for how they are feeling	Takes responsibility for their feelings and knows they can make themselves feel better
Dwells on their problems	Looks for solutions
Passively drifts	Pro-actively takes action
Feels pinned down	Feels free
Blames others	Empowers themselves
Talks about their past problems	Talks about their future
Gives up	Keeps going
Fears what life may bring	Enthused by what life may bring
Waits for life to happen	Makes life happen
Believes they have bad luck	Takes control of their life
Wants to know the outcome before having a go	Trusts their instinct on what feels right and goes for it
Feels powerless to change	Knows they have the power to think, feel or go in the direction they want
Is affected by others	Is resilient and lets others be
Wants others to be a certain way	Lets others be who they are
Believes happiness comes from external circumstances	Knows happiness comes from being themselves and following their dreams
Feels life has given them 'muck'	Uses the 'muck' to fertilise and grow in positive new directions

The Super Trooper mentality is a game changer.

Adopting a mindset that sees the best and most positive outcomes is one of the most important things we can do to improve our lives. It will also help raise us up The Happiness Barometer.

Our inner fire

It never ceases to amaze me that somewhere inside us all there is such a strong desire to never give up. Even in the most extreme circumstances when facing huge difficulties or feeling that all is lost, this inner strength is always there. It may only be a flicker rather than a burning fire in our bellies, but with a bit of nurturing it can be stoked up into the flame that lights up our inner fire again.

It is incredible the power this has in our lives.

In twenty years of working with clients, I have never met anyone who hasn't faced a big personal challenge of some kind in their lives. Everyone faces challenges and to overcome them we need to find our own inner power to help us out.

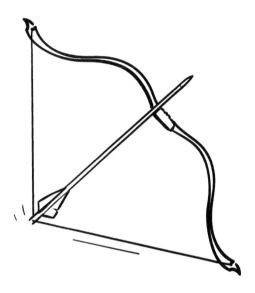

Consider the analogy of the archer pulling back the string on his bow. It is the backwards motion that creates the energy and power, which launches the arrow forwards. In the same way, whatever has happened in our lives, we can use the energy of our reaction to it to fire up our strength of spirit, and launch our lives forwards to a new and better place.

We can use this power to change things far more than we might imagine.

We may have been knocked down, but we don't have to be knocked out.

Take little steps. It is always possible to get back up again and move our lives forwards.

Turn your 'muck' to luck

Whilst Droopers believe that life has given them 'muck' (a bad situation) and they have no choice but to sit in it, Super Troopers work out ways to use that 'muck' as fertiliser to help them grow, in the same way that farmers use manure to give extra nourishment to the soil to help new life to flourish. Something seemingly bad, the 'muck', can be the catalyst for positive change.

Have you ever had a tough life experience, but as you came out the other side, you realised that it has given you a whole new perspective and understanding?

After getting through difficult times so many of my clients have looked back with a new perspective and said:

- They will do things differently now
- They see things differently now
- They are stronger in themselves now
- They embrace life differently now
- They make better choices now

- They find more happiness in small things now
- They have found a new direction or purpose in their lives because of what has happened

Using the 'muck' of a tricky situation can be the fertiliser to change. This fertiliser helps us see life through a whole new lens and we can grow and move forward as people because of it.

It is true that many difficult circumstances take us way out of our comfort zone, but it seems it is the difficulty itself which creates the new openings in our hearts and minds. In this way, the 'muck' becomes a useful focusing tool. It helps us focus towards thinking about what we really want in our lives, and on what is most important to us now.

Chances are, if we are in the middle of something big happening in our lives, we may not be able to see any good in our situation just now. However with a bit of water under the bridge, we may be able to look back at what we have learned from these tough times, and how we can use that to improve our lives in the future. This is how we turn our 'muck' to luck.

Asking, "What can I learn from this?" can make all the difference. Finding the good, even if it is only a small glimmer of light in the situation, helps creates a better, more empowered version of ourselves.

This changes our future in a big way. It helps take us back up The Happiness Barometer.

Here are some situations I have seen time and time again with my clients who, having been dolloped with 'muck', managed to turn it around and use the situation to help them grow as people instead.

	'Muck'	Growth
Job loss	Feel it is the end of their world, they are floored by the news	See it as a golden opportunity to find a new direction in life
Health problems	Believe they just have to live with their illness, maybe for the rest of their lives	Take action to improve their health and wellbeing by addressing any underlying factors that may have influenced the onset of their illness. Finding new alternative treatment methods if necessary
Losing a loved one	Feel overwhelmed by the sadness of losing someone they loved. They can still be struggling to deal with their loss years later	Realise over time that life is a precious gift and that their loved one would not want them to stop enjoying their life. They appreciate what they still have all the more, and live their life to the full
Breaking up with a partner	Feel bereft, believing that they can't go forwards in life on their own	See that the break up has created some time for them to develop and nurture a stronger sense of who they are and find out what makes them truly happy and fulfilled

Almost everyone will have experienced one or more of these unhappy life events. In learning how to make the best of what life throws at us, try answering this question:

Do I want to wallow in life's 'muck' or can I use it to help find a better future for myself?

Shifting our mindset from 'muck' to luck is a vital step on the road to a happier life.

The power of appreciation

When I first started out in practice, I remember going to visit a lady called Sally who was in her sixties. Two years earlier, she had woken up one night for a simple trip to the toilet. In the dark, as she walked across her landing, instead of turning into her bathroom she accidentally turned into the top of the staircase, and fell all the way to the bottom breaking her neck and leaving her permanently paralysed.

I remember being very nervous on my way to visit her, as I was expecting her to be incredibly sad. In fact what happened was the complete opposite. After relaying her story to me, she said that this had actually been one the best things that had ever happened to her.

Something inside her had fundamentally changed after the accident. She had found the time to appreciate life. She now keeps her windows open to the garden all day so she can listen to the bird song outside. She wonders at the brightness of the full moon. When people visit her she is a far better listener than she ever was before her accident. Even her sense of life's simple pleasures has improved, enabling her to appreciate a ripe piece of fruit or a scented rose so much more.

Before her life changed forever on that day, she had been constantly busy, and in too much of a hurry to appreciate anything. Since that day, as she adjusted to her new life she had found a deep appreciation of what is truly important in life. She was mentally far happier and more peaceful than she had ever been.

The experience of meeting Sally really humbled me. Not only had I made the huge mistake of trying to put myself in her shoes and wrongly imagining what she had been feeling, but it also showed me that you can never guess how someone else might be experiencing things. In that short meeting, I learned more about the power of appreciation than I had ever done before.

The power of appreciation is such an incredible tool. Appreciate all you can, every day. It is one of the quickest ways up The Happiness Barometer.

We can be happier if we learn to appreciate all that life has to offer

Life through a better lens

If we can learn to see things in a new and empowered way rather than through a murky and negative lens, things can only improve. It is knowing that we have a choice in how we respond and react to situations that makes the difference.

This may involve 'rolling with it' when small niggles arise day to day, or using our Super Trooper mindset to see the best in life and appreciating all that life has to offer. All of these should certainly enhance our ability to climb The Happiness Barometer.

If something more major happens which knocks us off course for a while, it is ok to sit, take stock and regroup. Then we must fire up as much inner power as we can manage and move forwards again. When the time is right, we can ask ourselves, "What did I learn from this and how can I use this new understanding to my advantage?"

By turning our 'muck' to luck we create a better and more empowered version of ourselves, and this is one of the most crucial ingredients to make sure that we don't get stuck in life.

WAY 6
Turn your 'muck' to luck

·BAROMETER RISING TIPS·

Make a choice to roll with
it whenever possible

Find your Super Trooper
mindset to see the best
outcomes and stay upbeat

Use your inner power
and don't give up

Learn from experiences to grow
and move forwards

Appreciate the wonders of life,
both big and small

Believe that you can find a
way to turn your 'muck' to luck

Pimp
up your
purpose

WAY 7

Whatever floats your boat

This is all about pointing our lives in the right direction. It is about finding what drives and excites us and makes us want to leap out of bed in the morning. Despite the fact that we can be or do whatever we want in life, we rarely just go for it. Consider these questions…

Does your life give you a buzz, a sense of fulfillment or a feeling of excitement?

Are you living a happy and contented life with the people you love?

Are you doing your dream job, loving going to work every day?

Are you engaged in activities that bring you fun, joy and happiness?

If the answer to some or all of the above is no, then something has gone wrong somewhere along the line. This is your life. Isn't it time to live it your way?

Doing what we love and are passionate about is a crucial part of the personal happiness journey. It is one of the building blocks to feeling good.

Getting what we want from our lives doesn't have to change the world, but starting to do what we love can and will certainly change our own world. It is not about making radical changes, quitting the nine to five and going to live on a desert island. It is more about taking simple steps to change the landscape of our day-to-day lives, until they become happier.

As I have mentioned several times now, I believe the answers always lie within us, so listening to how things make us feel is the most important aspect. It is about doing what you are passionate about and what makes you feel good. People often ask themselves, "What is my purpose?". I believe it boils down to one thing, doing what makes you feel good! There can be no greater joy than that.

The wrong soil

Imagine you are a houseplant which has been placed in the wrong type of soil, how are you going to get on? Chances are you aren't going to be able to grow very easily. Instead you may begin to wilt, lack energy and dry up. In the same way if we have planted ourselves in the wrong soil problems can arise. Over time we will notice problems developing in our wellbeing: physically, emotionally and mentally.

So what exactly do we mean by the wrong soil? It's a situation that you know is wrong for you. Perhaps you are in a relationship, job, place or home which doesn't feel right for you.

If we are able to identify the reason for being in the wrong soil then why do we stay put? Some common reasons I have seen for hanging around in the wrong soil are…

- Sticking with a habit
- Fear of moving on
- Believing that there's nothing better out there
- Holding onto status
- Fear of being lonely
- Not wanting to feel upset or to upset others
- Lacking the courage to make a move

Finding ourselves in the wrong soil creates an inner sadness, which can lead to frustration or to feeling low. After a while a general state of flatness can become normal and rather than living life we are just existing. This is a major sign that something has to change, so if this sounds familiar to you then it's time to make a change for the better... seek out your right soil wherever it may be.

One of my clients recently came to see me. She was a classic example of being in the wrong soil on two counts, she was very unhappy in her finance career and really not enjoying living abroad in Asia. She wanted to train as a nurse and move to the green and lush Welsh countryside to start a family with her fiancé. She was in the wrong place doing the wrong thing, which didn't suit who she really was. This took a toll on her health and she became weak with tiredness and inwardly frustrated. After she took steps to change things for the better both her health and her outlook improved.

Stagnation

S ometimes we are in the right soil but we have simply stagnated there. Stagnation means that there is no movement, no freshness or excitement in the situation. This can happen in relationships, at work or with life in general. In this instance a major external change probably isn't needed, more a subtle shift in attitude is what is required.

I have seen many clients who have walked away from their partners, their home, or their careers believing that they were in the wrong place, when in fact they were in the right place all along, but they just hadn't paid enough care and attention to maintaining and nurturing what they already had.

There is a subtle difference between being in the wrong soil which can only be fixed by making a significant change, and stagnating in the right soil which can be fixed by shifting perspective and taking more care. To solve stagnation we need to devote time, energy and commitment to the task at hand to liven it up again.

So now we know the problems… let's get to the good bit! How do we solve them? How do we make sure that we are in the right place, doing what we are passionate about and making progress towards a peaceful and happy life? Let's find out…

Activate the 3 Ps

1. PASSION

Big or small it doesn't matter

By finding and doing what we are passionate about in life, we create a buzz and energy inside. We don't have to make life-changing decisions to change our lives, we can start small. By beginning to do little things that create a better, more positive-feeling inside, we will move up The Happiness Barometer.

This could include taking up a hobby, getting creative, joining a club or dance class, getting active, playing a sport, drawing, writing, getting involved in an organisation or cause, becoming a karaoke king or queen... you can make your own list! Ask yourself...

What you could be doing that would make you feel really good?

How often are you doing things that you really love to do?

Each day? Once a week? Once a month?

If you don't usually have time for this kind of thing you need to make time! It is so important to your happiness levels that you do. Think outside the box and try something you have never done before. The more fun you can add to your life, the better you will feel.

Start small but start today. Find something which makes you happy and if it feels right to you, keep doing it.

If it is a bigger passion you feel driven to embrace, perhaps you want to make a career move or take on a big project, then this too is achievable. It may just take a bit more planning and time to bring it about, depending on your ability and resources to make it happen. The most important thing is to keep the idea at the forefront of your mind, and keep on trying to find ways to make it happen. It is really important to be in a good place mentally when we make these big decisions… more on this later.

I believe that everyone has an idea, skill or passion that they would love to take further and which they often daydream about. The more we follow these dreams and turn them into reality, the better we will feel.

Make sure it feels right

The key to engaging your passions is that whatever the activity or undertaking you choose, it has to feel right to you.

Often people drift along in other people's tides, following their parents' or partner's dreams instead of their own. Maybe they always wanted to work outdoors but family pressure led them to get an office job. Maybe a wife spends every weekend at motorbike rallies with her husband when she wishes she was going to craft fairs. It is very common to simply go along with what society, partners and parents expect of us. The worry is, what happens when we finally wake up twenty years later and realise that we have been following someone else's dream rather than our own?

If there are aspects of your life or work which you don't enjoy, it can be hard to see a way out whilst you are flat or disillusioned. The most important thing you can do in this situation is improve your mindset first.

The trick is to start moving in the direction you want to go, even if it is only mentally to begin with. By that I mean start thinking more about what you would like to be doing. Notice how you begin to feel. If you begin to feel better then you know you are going in the right direction. This is your internal guidance at work again.

There are two physical signs which I have noticed my clients display when they begin moving in the right direction…

1. Pingy eyes

When I'm with a client exploring various ideas about where they want to go next in their life, I look out for their pingy eyes.

"What the heck is "Pingy eyes?" you ask!

This is what happens to a person's eyes when they start talking about a topic that they are really passionate about, or hit upon what they want to do in life… their eyes light up, widen with excitement and begin to sparkle.

"There are the pingy eyes!" I say.

This is our body's physical reaction at the thought of heading in the right direction.

Try it out with your friends, ask them where they would like to go in their life; if anything were possible without being limited, what would they do? Then watch for the pingy eyes, it's their soul coming alive!

2. Bags of energy

The other key indicator is a person's energy level. When we are pointing in the right direction our energy levels surge. It may be only a little buzz or it might be a great blast of positive energy, but either way it will be there. This is a clever way in which our bodies help us to go in the direction our minds want.

Conversely, have you ever noticed an energy dip whilst doing things you don't want to do, or that at the mere thought of doing things you don't want to do, your energy is suddenly sapped?

Low energy is a common problem in the world these days. One of the main reasons for this is that many of us are not connected to what we want to be doing in our lives.

I have seen people who are in real slumps suddenly get loads of energy, once they find and begin to move in a direction they love.

2. PROGRESS

Invasion of the "Yes, buts"

Making progress is crucial. We must keep moving forwards in all aspects of our lives: relationships, work, home life, personal mindset, etc in order to be happy. Have you ever been stuck in a traffic jam and started to feel irritated, then once you began moving again you felt relief? The same goes for our lives. Negative feelings are often signs that we are not moving forwards.

All too commonly the "Yes, buts" get in the way. Have you ever had a conversation with someone, where they talked about what they would like to be doing, and you hatched some fantastic plans together… but then they came up with a load of "Yes, buts…"?

- I'm too old
- I'm too busy
- I'm not clever or qualified enough
- I'm not sure it will work
- I can't leave my job
- I haven't got the money
- What will people think?

The solution to all of these "Yes, buts" is to make what you want from life more important than all the uncertainties. A huge amount of happiness comes when you start to make progress in a direction that feels good and right to you.

As Pablo Picasso famously said,
"I am always doing that which I cannot do, in order that I may learn how to do it"

We need to do the same…

Not moving forwards in life is one of the main reasons why people don't get the life they want

Take inspired action

The best progress is made with inspired action. Inspired action is action arising from a good-feeling place in ourselves. Remember The Happiness Barometer and how when we are feeling good i.e. near the top of the barometer, we have better ideas and clearer thoughts?

I have found that if we take action when in this positive place, we have better outcomes in our lives.

Conversely actions taken when we are low on The Happiness Barometer will give a completely different outcome. Have you ever had a situation where you weren't feeling great and were in a bad mood, but you still took action from this negative place, either in words or deeds… ask yourself how well did it go? I find that conversations and actions taken whilst not feeling good rarely have a positive outcome.

Inspired actions are ideas that come from a good-feeling you. When we feel good we suddenly get great ideas, whether it is an urge to do something, phone someone, or visit somewhere. It's the best place for both creativity and productivity. I find that when we follow these inspired ideas, they are usually of enormous benefit.

This is why I always say to clients who are trying to find a new direction for their lives, "Let's get you feeling good first and then see what happens". As we feel better in ourselves, the right direction will become progressively clearer.

Sofa to success

One of my clients a few years ago was a lady who had multiple stresses in her life, she felt very low and that everything was a bit too much to handle. She was basically doing nothing with her life, apart from watching endless TV, whilst eating biscuits on the sofa. She came to see me and we talked about which direction she wanted to go in her life, and how we could 'pimp up her purpose' a little, as eating biscuits and watching TV didn't seem to be working very well for her.

She couldn't easily come up with what her passions

might be, but suggested that she could perhaps do some ironing for her friends and neighbours. I could tell that she wasn't thrilled by this idea, but at the same time it was a start and a step in the right direction to at least get her moving. We worked together for a few weeks on her self-belief and confidence, and gradually she began to feel better.

As she began to feel better and stronger in herself, the fog lifted and she suddenly knew exactly what she wanted to do... she absolutely loved jewellery and she became determined to do something to pursue this passion. The excitement of this idea improved her energy levels, and she soon signed herself up to a jewellery-making course.

She had to get to a place where she was feeling better in herself first, then the idea became clear. The jewellery idea was probably always somewhere in her head, but she had to clear the fog and learn to feel better before inspired action could show her the way.

Make sure that you are taking action from a good-feeling place; that's inspired action

Rev it up

Sometimes progress needs to be revved up.
If we are feeling stuck or simply want to get more excited about our futures, we can do this by imagining how we would like our perfect life to be. Try to really feel it, in all its glory… the sights, the sounds, the colours and how it would feel to be there.

What would your ideal life look like? Try to picture it in your mind.

Sometimes we need to literally 'rev it up' in our minds and get excited about where we want to go. Just as a car starts to move when we put revs on the rev counter, in the same way we can 'rev' ourselves up.

All the most successful people I have worked with have one thing in common; they knew where they wanted to get to and could visualise it. This knowledge carried them forwards, helping them to get through the hard times.

If we can shift our mindsets to stop thinking about all of the problems we are currently facing, and instead start thinking about how we would like things to be, we will feel a lot happier and make a lot more progress towards our goals.

Imagining how we would like our lives to be, creates a better feeling inside and is a great way to move up The Happiness Barometer.

Slotting into place

Once we start heading in the right direction life seems to have a funny way of helping us out, things just seem to slot into place. I couldn't even begin to count the number of my clients who would testify to this phenomenon! Perhaps they bumped into someone who was relevant to their new life's passion, or a fantastic offer was suddenly made to them. Whatever it may be, being on the right path draws in new opportunities.

People often become stressed and thrown off course, by believing they need to know exactly where and what they are aiming for in life. Sometimes we just have to allow for the fact that things may turn out differently to how we imagined. One of the biggest causes of stress is thinking that things are not working out as you imagined they would... instead learn to go with the flow and you will find that opportunities may arise in all sorts of different ways.

3. PEACEFULNESS

The missing 'peace' of the puzzle!

We have talked about pointing our lives in the right direction, doing things which we love to do and making progress, which is all very well and good, but we haven't yet mentioned one of the most important pieces needed to complete the puzzle of a happy life. That is peacefulness.

Sometimes we need to make ourselves feel good by simply being peaceful. Perhaps by watching a sunset, taking a walk, reading a book, just sitting quietly or enjoying ten minutes of meditation.

Take a moment to think about what makes you feel peaceful?

It sounds simple but it is surprising how stressful some people find being peaceful… they just can't do it. Not when there are text messages and emails to be sent, and Facebook, Twitter and Instagram feeds to be checked and updated! Our busy lives and constant mind chatter are not great for peacefulness. Think about how you can do a bit less Twittering about, and instead use that time to feel the real relaxation that the body and mind need to rejuvenate and self-heal.

I gave a talk about making progress as a way to become happier when someone asked me, "What about monks up in the Himalayas who just meditate all day. Are they not happy despite not making any progress?"

This was a great question, however my understanding is that monks are seeking a spiritual connection which they are continually deepening, so that is their progress. Also, being peaceful and quiet is a tool of inward reflection, allowing their bodies and minds to rest and re-charge.

Ask yourself how much time you spend feeling peaceful? If it isn't much, start making it a part of your life. It can be one of the most powerful states of mind we have. The striving and stress stops for a moment, whilst we allow our own gentle stillness within to come forward. People who can learn to feel this inner peacefulness are able to be more comfortable with themselves and have more personal resilience in their life.

Peacefulness allows us to calm our minds, helps the body to heal, replenishes our energy levels and offers more clarity allowing us to progress forwards.

Being peaceful may be just the tonic you are looking for.

Look at the stars, look how they shine for you

These words are a line from a very brilliant song, which was written by an old friend of mine who sings in a certain well-known rock band. When I hear that song it always reminds me of a valuable life lesson I learned from my children.

It was a dark, crisp and clear winter evening and two of my children, aged 5 and 7 at the time, were playing in the back garden. They kept on running inside saying, "Dad there's something amazing outside... come and look!".

But I was busy. The kind of busy that is not really busy, involving scrolling through emails I hadn't replied to and browsing social media.

At about the fourth time of asking they said, "Dad you can't miss this PLEASE come." So I begrudgingly put down my phone and followed them outside.

They got me to lie down on the grass and gaze straight up to the sky. It was a perfectly clear night and the sky was full as far as the horizon of incredible twinkling stars. "Look Dad!" they said, so excited, "Look at how amazing this is!".

I felt about an inch tall. The beauty of the sky was indeed amazing, they had never seen such a clear night sky packed with so many dazzling stars and they were mesmerised. The three of us lay side by side and began to pick out patterns in the sky, imagining what goes on out there in space. We were all lying on the cold, damp ground for ages, but in some ways this made us feel even more alive. This is such a precious memory for me.

Afterwards, I wondered at how I had almost missed out on this moment by inadvertently focusing on how 'busy' I was. This is not the only time that my children have reminded me of the peacefulness that is always there to be seen and experienced.

Enjoying the ride

As you pimp up your purpose and progress on your journey, try to find the right soil and plant yourself firmly in it. Try not to stagnate in any aspect of your life. Follow what feels right and makes you feel alive. Learn to take inspired action when you are riding high and enjoy the journey. Happiness is a combination of feeling happy in the present moment and being able to be excited about the future.

Let it unfold, roll with it and don't forget to enjoy the ride!

WAY 7
Pimp up your purpose

· BAROMETER RISING TIPS ·

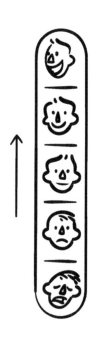

Do what you love and are passionate about

Plant yourself in the right soil

Notice when your pingy eyes and energy arrive

When you feel good that is the time to take positive action

Get excited about where you want to be in life

Find time to be peaceful with yourself and with the world

You are a happiness-generating machine

Go for it!

I hope you have enjoyed this book. I have certainly enjoyed writing it. It's been a really creative project for me, piecing together new ways to approach life and get the best from it. Wherever you are in life right now, remember to be gentle with yourself, there is no hurry, you will get there. As you take steps to move yourself up The Happiness Barometer, I would be willing to bet that you will experience what I call "The Invisible Magnet Effect" whereby good things which you have waited for and hoped would happen, begin to be drawn in towards you.

As you start to feel better in yourself, you will feel a whole new energy and joie de vivre, your perspective will be clearer and hopefully many aspects of your life will gain a new and positive momentum. The things, people and past situations which used to bother you, will begin to dissolve away. Life will not always run smoothly, new challenges lie ahead for us all, but once you learn that you can bounce back and make yourself feel good again, you are suddenly in control of your own happiness. This is what is so empowering.

By simply learning to feel better in yourself, you have the power to change things and alter the course of your life.

175

Think of the the book as I do; a friendly manual for when life throws us curve balls. Simply look back at different chapters for reminders of ways to make yourself feel better, as and when you feel the need.

As we mentioned right at the start of the book, finding the place that feels good, 'your natural state', is where your power lies. This 'good-feeling place' makes sure that you will continue to feel good no matter what. No matter what is going on around you, no matter what everyone else is doing or thinking and no matter what situation you are in.

When you can find your 'natural state' where you are being true to yourself and feeling at your best, then you have made it. You can stop believing that the grass is greener somewhere else, and instead realise that by using the 7 ways to life-changing happiness the power lies within you.

You can now

- **Fire up your own happiness**
  You are in charge of how happy you are and you can find ways to raise yourself up The Happiness Barometer.

- **Expose your Ta Daa**
  You can be the 'real you' again and live your life how you want to.

- **Tend your emotional garden**
  You can nurture and grow your own positive emotions, doing what it takes to feel your best and weeding out any negative emotions.

- **Jump on The Groovy Train of Thought**
  You can fill your mind with good-feeling happy thoughts and stop allowing it to get clogged up with negative ones.

- **Listen to your wise old gut**
  You can tune in and really listen to what your wise old gut is telling you because it always knows what is best.

- **Turn your 'muck' to luck**
  When something bad happens you can now see things from an empowered perspective, finding the best in people, situations and your future.

- **Pimp up your purpose**
  By doing what makes you feel good and discovering your passions, you will begin following the direction that feels best to you.

Once you learn to practice doing the above, you will be unstoppable, you will be your own happiness-generating machine!

People are far more centred and loving from this great-feeling place. It isn't selfish to feel good either, quite the opposite. By being the happiest person you can be, you become more loving, more creative, more energetic, more peaceful… in fact just more of everything good.

So say "Goodbye" to chasing the end of the rainbow, because the pot of gold which you thought was there was already within you.

Your happiness really is an 'Inside Job'.

Good luck on your journey and I wish you every success in creating your own very happy life… go for it!

'Notes to self'

Acknowledgements

Firstly I'd like to thank my wife Tasha, for her unwavering love, support and for being a magnificent sounding board when I have thrown yet another concept or idea at her. You reign me in and keep me on track!

This project would be nothing without the brilliance of Debs Syron. She has painstakingly edited each and every chapter. It's her diligence that has helped create such a wonderful book. So pleased you are up for the next project…

Denis, your designs and illustrations are amazing, I'm thrilled at how they have brought the book to life.

Jo, Frankie, Justine and Laura thank you for being my initial book shapers.

KPW, thank you for your attention to detail, I hope that the book cover colours are to your liking?

Thanks to Melody, Zeb and Marius who give me such inspiration.

Gini for the super photos that make me look half decent.

Mum you are the best of the best.

Rob and Theo thank you, and to all my extended family who have encouraged me to get to the finish line with this book, I made it!

Jay and Stef, the bet is on, the travel agent is on speed dial…!

Clare, thank you for letting me stay and write my book on your top floor. To the Swan at Streatley, for providing endless coffees and comfy seating.

To my many teachers: practitioners, lecturers, mentors and friends, thank you all for every nugget of wisdom you have lodged in my brain over the years. In particular: Jane Hurley, Richard Lang, Rosy Daniel, Ester Hicks, Mournir Tourabi, Helen Ford, Sandy C. Newbigging and to all the staff at COH Regents College, London who really got me going…

To my countless clients, from whom I have learnt so much over the last twenty years. Being witness to your journeys back to happiness has made my work-life so incredibly rewarding.

To my sponsor, your generosity in anonymously funding my college place in London twenty years ago launched my dream and set me on the path to writing this book. I can't thank you enough for changing my life, and in turn for helping others to change their lives too…

About the Author

As a practitioner, Matt bases himself in diverse clinics, some days on Harley Street, sometimes in his clients' offices, and on other days he can be found working in his man-shed in Oxfordshire; happiness can be found in many a different location!

His clients have included everyone from musicians, artists and film directors, to chief execs, nurses and students, who all had one thing in common; they wanted to make positive changes to their mindset and learn how to be happy again. Having given more than 15,000 consultations and witnessed many personal transformations, Matt knows what it takes to improve someone's state of mind, cast off their stresses and find their right direction.

A passionate speaker, Matt also lectures on happiness and wellbeing for medical teams at Great Ormond Street hospital. He loves giving his 'Pepp Talks' where he shares the essence of his book, motivating groups and organisations from all walks of life.

Matt was inspired to pursue natural routes to health and wellbeing by overcoming a chronic health condition in his teens. This was cured using homeopathic medicine when all conventional routes failed. A mysterious benefactor, who remains anonymous to this day, enabled him to train at the College of Homeopathy in London.

After graduating, Matt wanted to keep exploring the concept of happiness, both for himself and for his clients. A strong believer in the link between physical and mental health, he travelled the country and even sat on mountains to gain insights from counsellors, therapists and psychologists. Over time he has taken the many lessons he has learned, along with the ideas which felt good, to develop strategies for creating and maintaining a happy and healthy mind.

Under Matt's guidance, over the last twenty years countless people have transformed their outlook, cast off their stresses and, often after decades of unhappiness, finally found themselves living a new happier and more fulfilled life.

As an author and practitioner, living in Oxfordshire, England with his wife Tasha and children, Matt is thrilled to finally be able to share the secrets of everything he has learned.

Find out more about Matt and his Pepptalks at **www.mattpepper.com**

CPSIA information can be obtained
at www.ICGtesting.com
Printed in the USA
LVOW05s1220230118
563532LV00025B/582/P